WILLIAMS-SONOMA
PASTA COLLECTION

PASTA WITH SAUCES

WILLIAMS-SONOMA
PASTA COLLECTION

PASTA WITH SAUCES

GENERAL EDITOR
CHUCK WILLIAMS

RECIPES BY
MICHELE ANNA JORDAN

PHOTOGRAPHY BY
JOYCE OUDKERK POOL

WELDON OWEN

WILLIAMS-SONOMA
Founder: Chuck Williams

WELDON OWEN INC.
President: John Owen
Vice President and Publisher: Wendely Harvey
Managing Editor: Jill Fox
Recipe Analysis: Hill Nutrition Associates Inc.
    Lynne S. Hill, MS, RD; William A. Hill, MS, RD
Copy Editor: Carolyn Miller
Editorial Assistants: Stephani Grant, Marguerite Ozburn
Art Director: John Bull
Designer: Patty Hill
Production Director: Stephanie Sherman
Production Editor: Janique Gascoigne
Co-Editions Director: Derek Barton
Co-Editions Production Manager: Tarji Mickelson
Food Stylist: Susan Massey
Food Stylist Assistants: Andrea Lucich, Geri Lesko, Vicki Roberts-Russell
Prop Stylist: Carol Hacker
Photographer's Assistant: Myriam Varela
Hand Model: Tracey Hughes
Indexer: ALTA Indexing Service
Proofreaders: Desne Border, Ken DellaPenta
Illustrator: Nicole Kaufman
Writer's Photographer: David Licht
Props Courtesy: Biordi, Pottery Barn, Williams-Sonoma,
    Bryan's Meats, Cal-Mart
Special Thanks: Mick Bagnato, John Boland, James Carroll,
    Betty Ellsworth, Peggy Fallon, Leisel Hofman, Jane Lawrence,
    Ginny Stanford, Michel Stong, Jon Stong, Lesa Tanner

A Weldon Owen Production

First printing in 1996
10 9 8 7 6 5 4 3 2 1

Library of Congress
Cataloging-in-Publication Data:

Jordan, Michele Anna.
    Pasta with sauces / general editor, Chuck Williams ;
    recipes, Michele Anna Jordan ; photography by Joyce Oudkerk Pool.
    p. cm. — (Williams-Sonoma pasta collection)
    Includes index.
    ISBN 1-875137-07-6
    1. Cookery (Pasta)   I. Williams, Chuck.
    II. Title.   III. Series.
    TX809.M17J68 1996
    641.8'22—dc20   95-24284
                  CIP

All recipes include customary U.S. and metric measurements. Metric
conversions are based on a standard developed for this book and have
been rounded off. Actual weights may vary. Unless otherwise stated,
the recipes were designed for medium-sized fruits and vegetables.

Cover: Enjoy Classic Tagliolini with Pesto Sauce (recipe on page 59).

The Williams-Sonoma Pasta Collection
conceived and produced by Weldon Owen Inc.
814 Montgomery Street, San Francisco, CA 94133

In collaboration with Williams-Sonoma
3250 Van Ness Avenue, San Francisco, CA 94109

Production by Mandarin Offset, Hong Kong
Printed in China

CONTENTS

Sauced Pasta Basics 6

Enjoying Pasta with Sauces 8

Making Fresh Pasta 10   Cooking Perfect Pasta 16

Fresh Pasta Shapes 18

Fresh Pasta Noodles 38

Dried Pastas 68

Basic Terms and Techniques 118

Basic Recipes 124

Index 128

Sauced Pasta Basics

ENJOYING PASTA WITH SAUCES

It's the way almost all of us first learned to love pasta: boiled until tender but still chewy—al dente, as they say in Italy (see page 16)—then simply tossed with a flavorful sauce made on the stovetop. Whether that sauce was based on tomatoes, on cheese and cream or on a fragrant broth is really beside the point; the pasta made its impression, and those of us who have learned to love it keep coming back for more, however it might be prepared.

This book celebrates stovetop pasta dishes in all their many forms. You'll find recipes and instructions for making and shaping a wide range of fresh pastas, including colorful flavored varieties; for selecting and storing the many different kinds of dried pastas; and for cooking both fresh and dried pastas perfectly. All of this information, along with the Basic Terms and Techniques beginning on page 118, will enable you to prepare any of the recipes in this book with ease, as well as to gain the knowledge to create your own pasta dishes.

SERVING PASTA DISHES

The recipes in this book were designed to be served as main dishes, although most can be used as first courses or side dishes as well. Serve pasta with sauces piping hot. The best way to achieve this is to cook the sauce first, keeping it warm while you cook the pasta, and warm the bowls or plates in the oven before serving.

In most Italian homes, pasta is served from a large, wide, relatively shallow bowl that allows it to be tossed with ease. The pasta is then divided among individual bowls that are smaller versions of the serving vessel. The wide shape of the bowl makes it easy for diners to twirl strands of pasta onto forks, while helping to keep the pasta warm. Italian-style pasta bowls, both large and individually sized, may be found in any well-stocked kitchenware store.

That is not to say, however, that such dishware is absolutely essential. Pasta dishes may be served directly from any attractive serving bowl or platter. Shallow soup plates or standard dinner plates with a slightly raised rim will work well for serving individual portions of any recipes with sauces thick enough to cling to the pasta. For pasta in broth, use soup plates or standard soup bowls.

NUTRITIONAL ANALYSIS

Each recipe in this book has been evaluated by a registered dietitian. The resulting analysis lists the nutrient breakdown per serving. Use these numbers to plan nutritionally balanced meals. All ingredients listed with each recipe have been included in the analysis. Exceptions are items inserted "to taste" and those listed as "optional."

When seasoning with salt, bear in mind that each teaspoon of regular salt contains 2,200 mg of sodium. The addition of black or white pepper does not alter nutrient values. Substituted ingredients, recipe variations and accompaniments suggested in the recipe introductions or shown in the photographs have not been included in the analysis.

NUTRITIONAL TERMS

CALORIES (KILOJOULES)
Calories provide a measure of the energy provided by any given food. A calorie equals the heat energy necessary to raise the temperature of 1 kg of water by 1°Celsius. One calorie is equal to 4.2 kilojoules — a term used instead of calories in some countries.

PROTEIN
One of the basic life-giving nutrients, protein helps build and repair body tissues and performs other essential functions. One gram of protein contains 4 calories. A healthy diet derives about 15 percent of daily calories from protein.

CARBOHYDRATES
Classed as either simple (sugars) or complex (starches), carbohydrates are the main source of dietary energy. One gram contains 4 calories. A healthy diet derives about 55 percent of daily calories from carbohydrates, with not more than 10 percent coming from sugars.

TOTAL FAT
This number measures the grams of fat per serving, with 1 gram of fat equivalent to 9 calories, more than twice the calories present in a gram of protein or carbohydrate. Experts recommend that total fat intake be limited to a maximum of 30 percent of total daily calories.

SATURATED FAT
Derived from animal products and some tropical oils, saturated fat has been found to raise blood cholesterol and should be limited to no more than one-third of total daily fat calories.

CHOLESTEROL
Cholesterol is a fatty substance present in foods of animal origin. Experts suggest a daily intake of no more than 300 mg. Plant foods contain no cholesterol.

SODIUM
Derived from salt and naturally present in many foods, sodium helps maintain a proper balance of body fluids. Excess intake can lead to high blood pressure, or hypertension, in sodium-sensitive people. Those not sensitive should limit daily intake to about 2,200 mg.

FIBER
Dietary fiber aids elimination and may help prevent heart disease, intestinal disease and some forms of cancer. A healthy diet should include 20–35 grams of fiber daily.

$\mathcal{M}$AKING FRESH PASTA

Fresh pasta can be made at home using a food processor and a reasonably priced, manual pasta machine in about 10 minutes. The machine method is described in the instructions at right and shown in the step-by-step photographs on pages 12–13. Pasta can be made by hand as well (see page 13). Use the Egg Pasta recipes and the instructions at right as the basis for making all fresh pasta. To flavor the pasta, change the ingredients as noted for each variation.

PASTA INGREDIENTS

Semolina flour, "durum" in Italian, is made from the hardest wheat grown and is not bleached; for pasta making, be sure to purchase the finely ground variety, not coarse-ground semolina. The flour is high in gluten, which provides the elasticity necessary for kneading, cutting and shaping fresh pasta. All-purpose (plain) flour is a blend of wheat flours and has a finer feel than semolina flour. While fresh pasta can be made with only all-purpose flour, the addition of semolina flour gives the finished pasta a firmer texture.

Either common table salt or coarser kosher salt can be used when making fresh pasta. Use large eggs, which should be at room temperature to blend with the flour more easily.

Depending on the temperature and humidity of the kitchen, you may need to add some water when combining the ingredients so that the dough forms a ball properly. If the ball is too sticky, add more flour.

ONE-POUND PASTAS

Depending on the sauce, 1 lb (500 g) of pasta serves 4–6 as a main course or 6–8 as a first course or side dish.

EGG PASTA

1⅓ cups (7 oz/220 g) semolina flour

⅔ cup (4 oz/125 g) unbleached all-purpose (plain) flour plus additional for dusting

¼ teaspoon salt

2 eggs at room temperature

1½ tablespoons water

BASIL PASTA Increase the salt to ½ teaspoon, eliminate the water and add 3 tablespoons minced fresh basil.

BEET PASTA Increase the salt to ½ teaspoon, eliminate the water and add ⅓ cup (3 fl oz/80 ml) cooked beet purée.

OLIVE PASTA Increase the salt to ½ teaspoon, eliminate the water and add 2 tablespoons pitted Kalamata olive purée or commercial olive tapenade, oil drained.

PUMPKIN PASTA Increase the salt to ½ teaspoon, eliminate the water and add ⅓ cup (3 fl oz/80 ml) pumpkin purée and ⅛ teaspoon ground nutmeg.

Each recipe makes 1 lb (500 g)

Pasta with Sauces

POUND-AND-A-HALF PASTAS

Depending on the sauce, 1½ lb (750 g) of pasta serves 6–8 as a main course or 8–10 as a first course or side dish.

EGG PASTA

2   cups (10 oz/315 g) semolina flour

1   cup (5 oz/155 g) unbleached all-purpose (plain) flour plus additional for dusting

½   teaspoon salt

3   eggs at room temperature

3   tablespoons water

BASIL PASTA Replace the water with ¼ cup (½ oz/15 g) minced fresh basil.

BEET PASTA Replace the water with ½ cup (4 fl oz/125 ml) cooked beet purée.

BLACK PEPPER PASTA Add 1 tablespoon freshly ground pepper.

LEMON PASTA Replace the water with 1½ tablespoons fresh lemon juice and add 1 tablespoon grated lemon zest.

OLIVE PASTA Replace the water with 3 tablespoons pitted Kalamata olive purée or commercial olive tapenade, oil drained.

PUMPKIN PASTA Replace the water with ½ cup (4 fl oz/125 ml) pumpkin purée and ⅛ teaspoon ground nutmeg.

Each recipe makes 1½ lb (750 g)

MAKING PASTA BY MACHINE

1. In the work bowl of a food processor with the metal blade, combine all the ingredients. Pulse several times to incorporate.

2. Using a rubber spatula, scrape the sides of the work bowl. Pulse until the dough forms a ball. Add more water or flour, if necessary.

3. Remove the dough from the work bowl, dust it with flour to coat, cut the dough into 4–6 pieces and, using your hands, flatten them into rectangles. Set the rollers of a manual pasta machine to the widest setting. Working with 1 piece at a time, crank the dough through the machine, dust with flour, fold it in half lengthwise and crank it through again. Continue to dust, fold and pass the dough through the machine until it feels smooth and silky, 8–10 times. The dough should feel considerably drier than when you started and look paler in color. Do not be afraid of overhandling the dough; it benefits from lots of rolling. Repeat with the other pieces. Cover the dough with a kitchen towel and let rest for 1 hour at room temperature to relax the gluten.

4. Decrease the width of the roller opening by 1 notch. Working with 1 piece at a time, crank the dough through the machine twice, dusting with flour, as necessary. Reduce the roller opening by 1 notch and crank the dough through again. Continue reducing the roller opening and rolling the dough until the desired thickness is obtained (see page 15), 1/32 inch (1 mm)–1/16 inch (2 mm) for noodles and 1/64 inch (.5 mm) for shapes.

5. Sprinkle a wooden board or a counter lined with waxed paper with flour; do not work directly on laminate or tile to which pasta tends to stick. Place the pasta sheets on the flour and let rest until they are dry to the touch but pliant, about 10 minutes.

6. For shapes, cut the sheets according to the instructions beginning on page 14 or in the individual recipes. For noodles, install the cutting attachment onto the manual pasta machine and pass the sheets through.

MAKING PASTA BY MACHINE:
STEP-BY-STEP

1. PROCESSING THE INGREDIENTS
Gather the fresh pasta ingredients together (recipes on pages 10–11). In the work bowl of a food processor with the metal blade, combine all the ingredients. Pulse several times to incorporate.

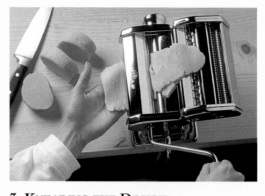

3. KNEADING THE DOUGH
Dust the dough ball with flour to coat and cut it into 4 pieces. Set the rollers of a manual pasta machine to the widest setting. Crank each piece of dough through the machine, dust it, fold it and pass it through again until it feels smooth and silky, 8–10 times. Cover and let rest for 1 hour.

2. FORMING THE DOUGH
Using a rubber spatula, scrape down the sides of the work bowl. Pulse several times for a few seconds until the dough forms a ball. If the dough does not form a ball, add water; if it is too sticky, add flour.

4. ROLLING THE DOUGH
Decrease the rollers of the pasta machine by 1 setting. Crank each piece of dough through the machine twice. Continue reducing the roller opening, dusting as necessary and rolling the dough through the machine until the desired thickness is obtained (see pages 14–15).

Pasta with Sauces

5. PREPARING TO CUT

Sprinkle a wooden board or a counter lined with waxed paper lightly with flour. Place the pasta sheets on the flour and let rest until they are dry to the touch but still pliant, about 10 minutes.

6. CUTTING THE PASTA

For shapes, cut the sheets according to the instructions beginning on page 14 or in the individual recipes. For noodles, install the cutting attachment onto the manual pasta machine and pass the sheets through.

MAKING PASTA BY HAND

1. MIXING THE DOUGH

On a work surface, combine the semolina and all-purpose flours and salt in a mound. Make a well in the center and break in the eggs. Add water or flavoring ingredients. Using a fork, blend the ingredients in the well, gradually drawing in the flour and enlarging the well until all the ingredients are combined into a dough.

2. KNEADING THE DOUGH

Dust a work surface with flour and transfer the dough to the surface. Using a dough scraper and the palm and heel of your hand, knead the dough, pushing it down and away from you and turning it repeatedly, until the dough feels smooth and satiny, 7–10 minutes; sprinkle on extra flour any time the dough becomes sticky or soft during kneading. Cut the dough into 4 equal pieces.

3. ROLLING THE DOUGH

Place a piece of dough on a floured work surface. With your hand, flatten it into a rectangle. Using a floured rolling pin, roll the dough away from you, applying moderate pressure. Turn the dough over and around. Repeat, adding flour if the dough becomes sticky, until the pasta reaches the desired thickness (see page 15), $\frac{1}{32}$ inch (1 mm)–$\frac{1}{16}$ inch (2 mm) for noodles and $\frac{1}{64}$ inch (.5 mm) for shapes.

4. PREPARING TO CUT

Line a table or counter with waxed paper or kitchen towels and sprinkle the paper or towels lightly with flour. Place the pasta sheets on the paper or towels side by side and let rest until they are dry to the touch but still pliant, about 10 minutes.

CUTTING FRESH PASTA

Whether you plan to make pasta shapes or noodles, begin by making the dough, following the recipes and instructions on the previous pages, up to the point at which the dough is ready to be cut. Follow the cutting and shaping instructions in individual recipes or below.

CUTTING PASTA SHAPES

Prepare the pasta according to the recipes and instructions on the previous pages. Transfer the pasta sheets to a floured work surface and cut following the instructions in the recipes or below.

QUADRUCCI Cut the pasta into 5-inch (13-cm) squares. Dust each square with flour and place in stacks of 3 or 4 squares. Cut the stacks into strips ½ inch (12 mm) wide, then cut the strips into ½-inch (12-mm) squares. Separate the squares and toss with flour to prevent sticking. Set on waxed paper. Dry 15–30 minutes before cooking.

MALTAGLIATI Cut the pasta into 5-inch (13-cm) squares. Dust each square with flour and place in stacks of 3 or 4 squares. Cut the stacks into diagonal pieces, changing the direction of the knife back and forth so that they form irregular triangles measuring about 1 inch (2.5 cm). Separate the triangles and toss with flour to prevent sticking. Set on waxed paper. Dry 15–30 minutes before cooking.

FAZZOLETTI Cut the pasta into 4-inch (10-cm) squares. Dust the squares with flour. Set on waxed paper. Dry at least 30 minutes before cooking.

GARGANELLI Cut the pasta into 1½-inch (4-cm) squares. Using a wooden pencil or a chopstick, roll each square diagonally around it, pressing slightly into the work surface to bond the pasta to itself. Slip the pasta off the pencil or chopstick and set on waxed paper. Dry 15–30 minutes before cooking.

FARFALLE Using a scalloped 2-inch (5-cm) cookie cutter, cut the pasta into circles. Pinch each round in the middle, pressing to keep in place. Set on waxed paper. Dry 15–30 minutes before cooking.

CUTTING NOODLES

Prepare the pasta according to the recipes and instructions on the previous pages. Roll the dough into sheets at the thickness shown on the opposite page.

To cut noodles using a pasta machine, secure the desired cutting attachment to the machine and crank the pasta through the cutter.

To cut pasta noodles by hand, transfer the pasta sheets to a floured work surface. Roll each sheet into a cylinder. Using a small, sharp knife, cut the cylinder crosswise at the width shown on the opposite page. Unroll the ribbons, dust with flour and set on waxed paper. Dry for 15 minutes before cooking.

PAPPARDELLE
1/32 inch (1 mm) thick
by 1¼ inch (3 cm) wide

FETTUCCINE
1/32 inch (1 mm) thick
by ¼ inch (6 mm) wide

TAGLIOLINI
1/32 inch (1 mm) thick
by ⅛ inch (3 mm) wide

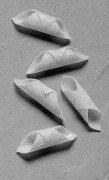

GARGANELLI
Tubes

TAGLIATELLE
1/16 inch (2 mm) thick
by ½ inch (12 mm) wide

LINGUINE
1/16 inch (2 mm) thick
by ⅛ inch (3 mm) wide

QUADRUCCI
Pasta Squares

FAZZOLETTI
Handkerchiefs

MALTAGLIATI
Triangles

FARFALLE
Butterflies

COOKING PERFECT PASTA

If you can boil water and tell time, you can cook perfect pasta. No special skills or equipment are required, and the method is the same whether the pasta you're cooking is fresh or dried.

It is customary to add salt to the boiling water prior to adding the pasta. For the best taste, use kosher salt, which is slightly coarser in texture. It does not contain the anti-caking additives found in refined table salt and imparts more flavor. However, if you're following a special sodium-restricted diet, you can leave out the salt completely without adversely affecting the finished dish.

EQUIPMENT NEEDED

For the best results when cooking pasta, choose a two-handled pot large enough to allow the pasta to float freely while cooking. This will help prevent the pasta from sticking together. Use a long-handled slotted spoon or cooking fork to stir the pasta as it cooks. A pasta fork, also called a pasta puller, is a long-handled plastic or wooden tool that looks like a flattened spoon with teeth; it is handy for lifting long pasta strands from the pot or serving bowl. Two thick pot holders or oven mitts and a sturdy colander that can withstand the heat of a large quantity of boiling water are also good investments for cooking pasta safely and successfully.

If you cook pasta frequently, consider investing a small amount of money in a special pasta pot, which includes a strainer insert that allows you to drain the pasta simply by lifting the insert from the pot, eliminating the need for pouring the pasta and its cooking water into a colander.

AL DENTE OR TENDER

The Italian term "al dente" has become universally accepted as a description of perfectly cooked pasta. Translated as "to the tooth," it describes pasta that offers a slight resistance to the bite, being tender but still chewy in texture. Technically, al dente is used only to describe the perfect cooked state of pasta that has been dried. Fresh pasta should be cooked just until "tender." In this case, tender means evenly soft but still chewy.

Either way, the best way to test for doneness is by biting into a single piece or strand of pasta. Use a slotted spoon or a long-handled cooking fork to fish it out of the boiling water.

Blow on the pasta briefly to cool it before biting into it. Dried pasta should be tender but firm and chewy. It should not show any white under-cooked portion at its center; al dente does not mean underdone. Fresh pasta should taste cooked, without any taste of flour.

COOKING PASTA: STEP-BY-STEP

1. BOILING THE WATER
Start with sufficient water in a large enough pot to allow the pasta to circulate freely. Over high heat, bring the water to a full, rolling boil. If desired, cover the pot to shorten the time needed to bring it to a boil.

3. BOILING THE PASTA
Cook the pasta, stirring occasionally, until it is al dente for dried, tender for fresh. Begin testing the pasta a minute or so before the earliest suggested time for doneness according to the recipes or the package directions.

2. ADDING SALT AND PASTA
When the water boils, add the salt. Adding the salt before the water boils may cause an unpleasant aftertaste. Shake off any excess flour from fresh pasta. Add the pasta, stirring to prevent it from sticking.

4. DRAINING THE PASTA
Set a sturdy colander in the sink. Protecting your hands with pot holders or oven mitts, carefully lift the pot and pour its contents into the colander. Lift and shake the colander until all the water has drained from the pasta. Do not rinse the pasta.

USING DRIED PASTA

The best dried pasta is manufactured entirely from semolina flour, which is ground from hard ("durum" in Latin) wheat. This variety of wheat is high in the elastic substance known as gluten, which gives the pasta its desired sturdiness. Mixed with water in the factory, the flour forms a paste that is extruded through metal dies to make strands, ribbons, tubes and other shapes, including those used in this book. The pasta is dried in chambers that carefully control humidity and temperature.

Once you have opened a package, store dried pasta in a tightly covered glass container in a cool, dark place. Use it within 1 year of purchase.

Cook dried pasta in the same manner as fresh pasta, although the cooking time will be longer. Once the dried pasta has cooked to al dente and been drained, it is usually necessary to toss it immediately with olive oil to coat lightly, which prevents sticking. Use about 1 tablespoon of extra-virgin olive oil per 1 lb (500 g) of pasta.

Sauced Pasta Basics

Fresh Pasta Shapes

WINDOWPANE PASTA WITH NASTURTIUM BUTTER

The windowpane effect is achieved by sealing parsley leaves between two sheets of fresh pasta rolled so thinly they are nearly translucent. Edible violas and nasturtiums provide a colorful garnish.

1　lb (500 g) Egg Pasta *(recipe on page 10)*

4　tablespoons (2 oz/60 g) Nasturtium Butter *(recipe on page 127)* at room temperature

60　fresh flat-leaf (Italian) parsley leaves

3　tablespoons fine yellow cornmeal

6　qt (6 l) water

1　tablespoon salt

⅓　cup (1½ oz/45 g) freshly grated Parmesan cheese

　　Edible violas

　　Nasturtium flowers and leaves

1. Make the Egg Pasta and roll it into sheets 4½ inches (11 cm) wide and 20 inches (50 cm) long. Make the Nasturtium Butter.
2. On a work surface, place a strip of pasta and cut it in half crosswise. Arrange the parsley leaves in 2 rows on top of 1 sheet of pasta, spacing about 1 inch (2.5 cm) between leaves. Moisten the edge of the pasta slightly with water. Place the other sheet of pasta on top of the moistened one and press them together gently. Using a rolling pin or a manual pasta machine at the narrowest setting, roll the pasta until it is nearly translucent and the parsley leaves are visible. Both the pasta and leaves will stretch considerably.
3. Using a serrated pastry cutter, cut the pasta into 2-inch (5-cm) squares, trimming the outer edges as well as cutting between the squares. Set the completed squares on a sheet of waxed paper or a kitchen towel and sprinkle with the cornmeal. Repeat with the remaining pasta to make 60 squares. Dry slightly before cooking, 15–30 minutes.
4. In a large pot over high heat, bring the water to a boil. Add the salt and the pasta squares and cook, stirring frequently so they do not stick together, until they are tender, about 2 minutes. Drain carefully.
5. In a large warmed bowl, combine the pasta squares and 2 tablespoons of the Nasturtium Butter and toss gently.
6. To serve, arrange 10 squares on individual warmed plates. Top with an equal amount of the remaining Nasturtium Butter, Parmesan cheese, edible violas and nasturtium flowers and leaves. Serve hot.

Serves 6

NUTRITIONAL ANALYSIS: Calories 330 (Kilojoules 1,385); Protein 11 g; Carbohydrates 44 g; Total Fat 12 g; Saturated Fat 6 g; Cholesterol 96 mg; Sodium 674 mg; Dietary Fiber 2 g

Pasta with Sauces

CRAB AND GARLIC BUTTER OVER FARFALLE

Don't pass up this delicate dish just because handmade farfalle seem time-consuming. Once the fresh pasta is made, shaping and drying the butterflies doesn't take long. Of course, dried farfalle may be used instead.

1½ lb (750 g) Lemon Pasta *(recipe on page 11)*

⅓ cup (3 oz/90 g) unsalted butter

1 tablespoon minced garlic

1 tablespoon hot pepper sauce

2 tablespoons minced fresh flat-leaf (Italian) parsley

2½ cups (15 oz/450 g) freshly cooked crabmeat

 Salt

8 qt (8 l) water

1½ tablespoons salt

1 lemon, cut into 8 wedges

1. Make the Lemon Pasta and shape it into farfalle (see pages 14–15).
2. In a saucepan over medium heat, melt the butter. Add the garlic and hot pepper sauce and simmer for 2 minutes. Remove from the heat and add the parsley, crabmeat and salt to taste.
3. In a large pot over high heat, bring the water to a boil. Add the 1½ tablespoons salt and the farfalle and cook until tender, about 2 minutes. Drain well.
4. In a large warmed bowl, combine the farfalle and crab mixture. Toss to mix well.
5. To serve, divide among individual warmed plates. Garnish with a lemon wedge. Serve hot.

Serves 8

NUTRITIONAL ANALYSIS: Calories 347 (Kilojoules 1,457); Protein 20 g; Carbohydrates 41 g; Total Fat 11 g; Saturated Fat 5 g; Cholesterol 153 mg; Sodium 615 mg; Dietary Fiber 2 g

Fresh Pasta Shapes

POTATO GNOCCHI WITH SUMMER TOMATO SAUCE

These classic dumplings go very well with a wide variety of sauces. Try them with Pesto Sauce, Salsa Verde (recipes on page 125) or any other one that strikes your fancy.

1³⁄₄ cups (14 fl oz/430 ml) Summer Tomato Sauce *(recipe on page 124)*

2 lb (1 kg) russet potatoes

2 egg yolks, lightly beaten

4 teaspoons salt

2 cups (10 oz/315 g) all-purpose (plain) flour

4 qt (4 l) water

1. Make the Summer Tomato Sauce. Preheat an oven to 375°F (190°C).
2. Using a fork, puncture the potatoes in several places and bake until tender, about 1 hour. Cool until easy to handle.
3. Peel the potatoes, cut them into chunks, place in a bowl and mash them. Add the egg yolks and 2 teaspoons of the salt. Add the flour, ¹⁄₂ cup (2¹⁄₂ oz/75 g) at a time, mixing just until the dough is smooth but still just slightly sticky (some potatoes will take more flour than others). Divide the dough into pieces about the size of a tennis ball.
4. On a floured surface, form each piece of dough into a rope about ³⁄₄ inch (2 cm) thick. Cut each rope into ³⁄₄-inch (2-cm) pieces. Place one piece at a time on the inside curve of a fork. With the tip of the index finger pointing directly perpendicular to the fork, press the piece of dough against the prongs. While still pressing, flip it away from the prongs, toward the fork handle. Let it roll off and drop to the work surface.
5. In a large pot over high heat, bring the water to a boil. Add the remaining 2 teaspoons salt and the gnocchi in batches. When they float to the surface, cook for an additional 15 seconds. Using a slotted spoon, transfer to a large warmed bowl. Drain any water collected in the bowl. Add the Summer Tomato Sauce and toss gently.
6. To serve, divide among individual warmed plates. Serve hot.

Serves 6

NUTRITIONAL ANALYSIS: Calories 302 (Kilojoules 1,268); Protein 8 g; Carbohydrates 61 g; Total Fat 2 g; Saturated Fat 1 g; Cholesterol 71 mg; Sodium 1,135 mg; Dietary Fiber 4 g

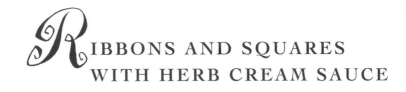 

RIBBONS AND SQUARES WITH HERB CREAM SAUCE

The combination of colors and shapes in this dish is both whimsical and delicious, well justifying the time it takes to prepare the pasta. The little squares are called quadrucci *in Italian.*

1 lb (500 g) Beet Pasta *(recipe on page 10)*

1 lb (500 g) Pumpkin Pasta *(recipe on page 10)*

¼ cup (2 fl oz/60 ml) plus 8 qt (8 l) water

1½ tablespoons salt

1 tablespoon extra-virgin olive oil
Salt and freshly ground pepper

HERB CREAM SAUCE

2 cups (16 fl oz/500 ml) heavy (double) cream

2 flat-leaf (Italian) parsley sprigs

2 fresh thyme sprigs

2 fresh oregano sprigs

2 fresh marjoram sprigs

¾ cup (3 oz/90 g) freshly grated aged Asiago cheese
Salt and freshly ground pepper

1. Make the Beet Pasta and the Pumpkin Pasta.
2. On a work surface, place a strip of Beet Pasta, brush lightly with some of the ¼ cup (2 fl oz/60 ml) water and top with a strip of Pumpkin Pasta. Using a rolling pin or a mechanical pasta maker on the narrowest setting, press the two pieces of pasta together, securing them firmly so that they become one sheet, beet on one side, pumpkin on the other. Cut all but 1 sheet into tagliatelle (see pages 14–15). Cut the remaining sheet into quadrucci (see pages 14–15).
3. Prepare the Herb Cream Sauce (see below).
4. In a large pot over high heat, bring the 8 qt (8 l) water to a boil. Add the salt and the tagliatelle and cook for 1 minute. Add the quadrucci and cook until tender, about 2 minutes. Drain well, place in a large warmed bowl and toss immediately with the olive oil.
5. To serve, divide the tagliatelle and quadrucci among individual warmed plates. Top with an equal amount of the Herb Cream Sauce and salt and pepper to taste.

HERB CREAM SAUCE

1. In a medium saucepan over medium heat, simmer the cream and the herb sprigs until the cream is reduced by one-third. Remove from the heat and steep for 10 minutes. Remove and discard the herb sprigs.
2. Place over medium-low heat. Add the Asiago cheese and salt and pepper to taste. Cook, stirring constantly, until the cheese is completely melted. Keep warm until ready to use.

Serves 8

NUTRITIONAL ANALYSIS: Calories 591 (Kilojoules 2,481); Protein 17 g; Carbohydrates 61 g; Total Fat 30 g; Saturated Fat 17 g; Cholesterol 195 mg; Sodium 745 mg; Dietary Fiber 3 g

 Fresh Pasta Shapes

PUMPKIN SQUARES AND SWISS CHARD SOUP

A simple soup like this one benefits greatly from a flavorful homemade stock. Fresh pasta cut into little square shapes are called quadrucci *in Italian.*

1 lb (500 g) Pumpkin Pasta *(recipe on page 10)*

8 cups (64 fl oz/2 l) Chicken Stock *(recipe on page 126)*

1 lb (500 g) fresh Swiss chard (silverbeet), large stems removed

2 tablespoons olive oil

1 teaspoon minced garlic
   Salt and freshly ground pepper

6 qt (6 l) water

1 tablespoon salt

⅓ cup (1½ oz/45 g) freshly grated Parmesan cheese

1. Make the Pumpkin Pasta and cut it into quadrucci (see pages 14–15).
2. In a medium pot over low heat, bring the Chicken Stock to a simmer.
3. On a work surface, cut the chard crosswise into 1-inch (2.5-cm) strips. In a medium frying pan or wok over medium heat, heat the olive oil. Add the garlic and sauté for 1 minute. Add the chard and sauté, stirring frequently, until it is wilted, about 5 minutes. Add the salt and pepper to taste. Keep warm.
4. In a large pot over high heat, bring the water to a boil. Add the 1 tablespoon salt and the quadrucci and stir vigorously to separate the small pieces of pasta. Cook until tender, about 2 minutes. Drain well.
5. To serve, divide the quadrucci among individual warmed soup bowls. Top with an equal amount of the chard, stock and Parmesan cheese. Serve hot.

Serves 6

NUTRITIONAL ANALYSIS: Calories 331 (Kilojoules 1,392); Protein 16 g; Carbohydrates 45 g; Total Fat 12 g; Saturated Fat 3 g; Cholesterol 76 mg; Sodium 878 mg; Dietary Fiber 2 g

OLIVE PASTA TUBES WITH ANCHOVIES AND TOMATOES

This tangy sauce is a fresh version of the traditional Italian puttanesca *sauce. It is both beautiful and delicious with these hand-rolled pasta shapes called* garganelli *in Italian, but you may also use dried penne.*

1 lb (500 g) Olive Pasta *(recipe on page 10)*

3 tablespoons extra-virgin olive oil

1 teaspoon minced garlic

4 anchovy fillets in olive oil, drained and chopped

2 cups (12 oz/375 g) cherry tomatoes, cut into quarters

1 cup (5 oz/155 g) Kalamata olives, pitted and sliced

2 tablespoons capers, drained

2 tablespoons minced fresh flat-leaf (Italian) parsley

  Red pepper flakes

  Salt

6 qt (6 l) water

1 tablespoon salt

1. Make the Olive Pasta and cut it into garganelli (see pages 14–15).
2. In a medium frying pan over medium-low heat, heat the olive oil and sauté the garlic and anchovies for 2 minutes. Add the tomatoes, olives and capers and cook until the ingredients are just heated through, 3–4 minutes. Add the parsley and red pepper flakes and salt to taste. Keep warm.
3. In a large pot over high heat, bring the water to a boil. Add the 1 tablespoon salt and the garganelli and cook until tender, about 4 minutes. Drain well.
4. In a large warmed bowl, combine the garganelli and three quarters of the tomato mixture. Toss to mix well.
5. To serve, divide among individual warmed plates. Top with an equal amount of the remaining tomato mixture. Serve hot.

Serves 6

NUTRITIONAL ANALYSIS: Calories 360 (Kilojoules 1,510); Protein 10 g; Carbohydrates 45 g; Total Fat 16 g; Saturated Fat 2 g; Cholesterol 72 mg; Sodium 1,048 mg; Dietary Fiber 3 g

Fresh Pasta Shapes

PASTA HANDKERCHIEFS WITH TOMATO AND BUTTER SAUCE

This version of pasta handkerchiefs — fazzoletti in Italian — was designed for entertaining. The sauce may be made one or two days in advance and reheated. A simpler dried broad noodle may be substituted.

1 lb (500 g) Egg Pasta *(recipe on page 10)*

6 tablespoons (3 oz/90 g) unsalted butter

½ yellow onion, peeled and finely chopped

2½ lb (1.25 kg) plum (Roma) tomatoes, peeled, seeded and chopped *(see page 124)*
Salt and freshly ground pepper

6 qt (6 l) water

1 tablespoon salt

2 tablespoons minced fresh flat-leaf (Italian) parsley

¾ cup (3 oz/90 g) freshly grated Parmesan cheese

1. Make the Egg Pasta and cut it into 30 fazzoletti (see pages 14–15).

2. To make the tomato and butter sauce, in a large frying pan over medium-low heat, melt 3 tablespoons of the butter until it foams. Add the onion and sauté until the onion is translucent, about 8 minutes. Add the tomatoes, reduce the heat to low and simmer until most of the liquid in the tomatoes has evaporated, about 15 minutes. Cut the remaining 3 tablespoons butter into small pieces and whisk them into the tomatoes. Add salt and pepper to taste. Keep warm.

3. In a large pot over high heat, bring the water to a boil. Add the 1 tablespoon salt, 5 fazzoletti at a time, and cook until tender, about 3 minutes. Using a slotted spoon, carefully remove each fazzoletto, drain it quickly and dip it into the sauce so that each side is thinly coated. Fold each fazzoletto in half diagonally, then fold it again so that it forms a small triangle.

4. To serve, arrange 3 fazzoletti on individual warmed plates, working very quickly so that they do not get cold. Top with an equal amount of the tomato and butter sauce, parsley and Parmesan cheese. Serve hot.

Serves 10

NUTRITIONAL ANALYSIS: Calories 206 (Kilojoules 865); Protein 8 g; Carbohydrates 24 g; Total Fat 9 g; Saturated Fat 5 g; Cholesterol 56 mg; Sodium 308 mg; Dietary Fiber 2 g

$\mathscr{P}$ASTA TRIANGLES WITH TOMATOES AND BASIL

Cutting this pasta into perfect little triangles, called maltagliati *in Italian, and pairing it with quartered cherry tomatoes gives this dish its strong visual appeal.*

1½ lb (750 g) Basil Pasta *(recipe on page 11)*
¼ cup (2 fl oz/60 ml) extra-virgin olive oil
1 tablespoon minced garlic
1½ lb (750 g) cherry tomatoes, cut into quarters
8 qt (8 l) water
1½ tablespoons salt
¼ cup (¼ oz/7.5 g) fresh basil leaves, cut into thin strips
⅓ cup (1½ oz/45 g) freshly grated aged Asiago cheese
Fresh basil sprigs

1. Make the Basil Pasta and cut it into maltagliati (see pages 14–15).
2. In a large frying pan over low heat, heat the olive oil. Add the garlic and sauté until tender, about 2 minutes. Add the tomatoes and sauté, stirring gently, until just heated through, about 3 minutes. Keep warm.
3. In a large pot over high heat, bring the water to a boil. Add the salt and the maltagliati and stir vigorously to separate the pieces. Cook until tender, about 2 minutes. Drain well.
4. In a large warmed bowl, combine the maltagliati, half of the cherry tomatoes and all of the basil strips. Toss to mix well.
5. To serve, place on individual warmed plates. Top with an equal amount of the remaining tomatoes and Asiago cheese. Garnish with a basil sprig. Serve hot.

Serves 8

NUTRITIONAL ANALYSIS: Calories 327 (Kilojoules 1,374); Protein 11 g; Carbohydrates 45 g; Total Fat 11 g; Saturated Fat 3 g; Cholesterol 83 mg; Sodium 521 mg; Dietary Fiber 3 g

Fresh Pasta Shapes

$\mathcal{S}$AGE SQUARES WITH SAGE AND SHALLOT BUTTER

Here, fresh sage leaves are sealed between sheets of pasta to lovely effect. The dish makes an elegant first course before a traditional autumn main course such as roast turkey.

1 lb (500 g) Egg Pasta *(recipe on page 10)*

¼ cup (2 oz/60 g) Sage and Shallot Butter *(recipe on page 127)* at room temperature

¼ cup (2 fl oz/60 ml) plus 6 qt (6 l) water

60 fresh sage leaves, 1–1½ inches (2.5–4 cm) long

2 teaspoons cornmeal

1 tablespoon salt

2 tablespoons minced fresh sage

1. Make the Egg Pasta and roll it into sheets 4½ inches (11 cm) wide and 20 inches (50 cm) long. Make the Sage and Shallot Butter.
2. On a work surface, place a strip of pasta and cut it in half crosswise. Using a pastry brush, coat the surface of 1 strip with some of the ¼ cup (2 fl oz/60 ml) water. Arrange the sage leaves in 2 rows on top of the moistened sheet of pasta, spacing about 1 inch (2.5 cm) between leaves. Place the other half sheet of pasta on top of the moistened one and press them together gently. Using a rolling pin or manual pasta machine at the narrowest setting, roll the pasta until it is nearly translucent and the sage leaves are visible. Both the pasta and the leaves will stretch considerably.
3. Using a pasta cutter, cut the pasta into 60 2-inch (5-cm) squares, trimming the outer edges as well as cutting between the squares. Set the completed squares on waxed paper or kitchen towels and sprinkle with the cornmeal. Dry slightly before cooking, 15–30 minutes.
4. In a large pot over high heat, bring the 6 qt (6 l) water to a boil. Add the salt and the pasta squares and cook, stirring frequently so they do not stick together, until tender, about 2 minutes. Drain carefully.
5. In a large warmed bowl, combine the pasta squares and the Sage and Shallot Butter and toss gently.
6. To serve, arrange 10 squares on individual warmed plates. Top with an equal amount of the minced sage. Serve hot.

Serves 6

NUTRITIONAL ANALYSIS: Calories 306 (Kilojoules 1,285); Protein 9 g; Carbohydrates 40 g; Total Fat 12 g; Saturated Fat 7 g; Cholesterol 97 mg; Sodium 486 mg; Dietary Fiber 2 g

Pasta with Sauces

Fresh Pasta Noodles

PUMPKIN TAGLIATELLE WITH GORGONZOLA SAUCE

Although pumpkin pasta may be best served in the autumn, when its color and aroma resonate with the season, you can make this dish year-round using canned pumpkin in the pasta.

1½ lb (750 g) Pumpkin Pasta *(recipe on page 11)*

2 cups (16 fl oz/500 ml) heavy (double) cream

7 fresh rosemary sprigs

6 oz (185 g) Gorgonzola cheese, crumbled

Salt and freshly ground pepper

8 qt (8 l) water

1½ tablespoons salt

1. Make the Pumpkin Pasta and cut it into tagliatelle (see pages 14–15).

2. To make the Gorgonzola sauce, in a medium saucepan over medium heat, bring the cream and 1 of the rosemary sprigs to a boil, reduce the heat to low and simmer until the cream is reduced by one-third, about 15 minutes. Remove from the heat. Remove and discard the rosemary sprig.

3. Stir in the Gorgonzola cheese. Reduce the heat to low, return the pan to the heat and stir until the cheese is completely melted. Add salt and pepper to taste. Remove from the heat but keep warm.

4. In a large pot over high heat, bring the water to a boil. Add the 1½ tablespoons salt and the tagliatelle and cook until tender, about 2 minutes. Drain well.

5. In a large warmed bowl, combine the tagliatelle and the Gorgonzola sauce. Toss to mix well.

6. To serve, divide among individual warmed plates. Garnish with the remaining rosemary. Serve hot.

Serves 8

NUTRITIONAL ANALYSIS: Calories 506 (Kilojoules 2,126); Protein 14 g; Carbohydrates 43 g; Total Fat 32 g; Saturated Fat 19 g; Cholesterol 180 mg; Sodium 767 mg; Dietary Fiber 2 g

CHICKEN AND FETTUCCINE WITH TOMATO CREAM SAUCE

The chicken and the cream sauce are prepared very quickly to make this satisfying main course. If you don't have enough time to prepare the fresh pasta, substitute dried egg or spinach fettuccine.

1½ lb (750 g) Tomato Pasta *(recipe on page 11)*

1 tablespoon pure olive oil

2 whole chicken breasts (2½ lb/ 1.25 kg), boned, skinned and cubed

Salt and freshly ground pepper

8 qt (8 l) water

1½ tablespoons salt

6 sun-dried tomatoes packed in oil, drained and cut into strips

Fresh thyme sprigs

TOMATO CREAM SAUCE

1½ cups (12 fl oz/375 ml) heavy (double) cream

1 fresh thyme sprig

1 cup (8 fl oz/250 ml) Chicken Stock *(recipe on page 126)*

10 sun-dried tomatoes packed in oil, puréed

Salt and freshly ground pepper

½ teaspoon fresh thyme leaves

1. Make the Tomato Pasta and cut it into fettuccine (see pages 14–15). Prepare the Tomato Cream Sauce (see below).

2. In a sauté pan or a wok over medium heat, heat the olive oil. Add the chicken and sauté, turning frequently, until it is cooked through, 7–8 minutes. Add the salt and pepper to taste. Remove from the heat and keep warm.

3. In a large pot over high heat, bring the water to a boil. Add the 1½ tablespoons salt and the fettuccine and cook until tender, about 2 minutes. Drain well.

4. In a large warmed bowl, combine the fettuccine and Tomato Cream Sauce. Toss to mix well.

5. To serve, divide among individual warmed plates. Top with an equal amount of the chicken and tomatoes. Garnish with a thyme sprig. Serve hot.

TOMATO CREAM SAUCE

1. In a heavy, medium saucepan over medium heat, bring the cream and thyme sprig to a boil. Lower the heat and simmer until the cream is reduced by one-third, about 10 minutes. Remove from the heat and let sit 10 minutes.

2. Remove and discard the thyme sprig. Return the cream to the heat, add the Chicken Stock and simmer for 5 minutes. Add the tomato purée and salt and pepper to taste. Remove from the heat, stir in the thyme leaves and keep warm until ready to use.

Serves 8

NUTRITIONAL ANALYSIS: Calories 764 (Kilojoules 3,206); Protein 34 g; Carbohydrates 54 g; Total Fat 47 g; Saturated Fat 15 g; Cholesterol 194 mg; Sodium 614 mg; Dietary Fiber 6 g

Fresh Pasta Noodles

BLACK PEPPER LINGUINE WITH RADICCHIO AND PANCETTA

Make this dish with dried linguine if time is limited. You can also replace the pancetta with regular bacon taking care to drain off excess fat after the bacon has been cooked.

1½ lb (750 g) Black Pepper Pasta *(recipe on page 11)*

1 lb (500 g) radicchio

2 tablespoons extra-virgin olive oil

8 oz (250 g) pancetta, diced

½ cup (4 fl oz/125 ml) white wine vinegar

4 tablespoons (2 oz/60 g) unsalted butter

8 qt (8 l) water

1½ tablespoons salt

6 oz (185 g) fresh goat cheese, crumbled

Salt

⅓ cup (3 oz/90 g) pine nuts, toasted *(see page 121)*

1. Make the Black Pepper Pasta and cut it into linguine (see pages 14–15).
2. To prepare the radicchio, remove any wilted outer leaves, cut each head in half and cut out and discard the cores. Cut the radicchio crosswise into pieces ½ inch (12 mm) wide.
3. In a heavy frying pan over medium heat, heat the olive oil. Add the pancetta and cook until just crisp, about 10 minutes. Add the radicchio and vinegar and cook covered, until the radicchio is completely wilted, about 5 minutes. Remove the lid and simmer until the liquid is reduced by half, about 3 minutes. Stir in the butter and remove from the heat.
4. In a large pot over high heat, bring the water to a boil. Add the 1½ tablespoons salt and the linguine and cook until tender, about 2 minutes. Drain well.
5. In a large warmed bowl, combine the linguine, pancetta mixture, goat cheese and salt to taste. Toss to mix well.
6. To serve, divide among individual warmed plates. Top with an equal amount of the pine nuts. Serve hot.

Serves 8

NUTRITIONAL ANALYSIS: Calories 549 (Kilojoules 2,306); Protein 21 g; Carbohydrates 46 g; Total Fat 33 g; Saturated Fat 14 g; Cholesterol 128 mg; Sodium 885 mg; Dietary Fiber 4 g

TAGLIOLINI WITH ASPARAGUS AND ZUCCHINI

The trick to achieving excellent results with this dish is to cook the asparagus and the bell peppers (capsicums) long enough to draw out their flavors while cooking the zucchini (courgettes) briefly to retain their firm texture.

1½ lb (750 g) Egg Pasta
   (recipe on page 11)

¼ cup (2 fl oz/60 ml) Brown Butter
   (recipe on page 126)

2 red bell peppers (capsicums),
   halved lengthwise, stemmed,
   seeded and deribbed *(see page 123)*

1 lb (500 g) fresh asparagus

2 small zucchini (courgettes)

1 tablespoon minced fresh ginger

1 teaspoon minced garlic
   Salt and freshly ground pepper

8 qt (8 l) water

1½ tablespoons salt

1. Make the Egg Pasta and cut it into tagliolini (see pages 14–15). Make the Brown Butter.

2. Cut each pepper into strips ¼ inch (6 mm) wide. Cut the strips in half. Cut the asparagus into pieces about 2½ inches (6 cm) long. If the stalks are particularly thick, cut them in half lengthwise. Slice each zucchini lengthwise into ribbons ¼ inch (6 mm) thick, then slice each ribbon into strips ¼ inch (6 mm) wide. Cut the strips into pieces 2½ inches (6 cm) long.

3. In a medium frying pan over low heat, heat the Brown Butter. Add the ginger and garlic and sauté for 2 minutes. Increase the heat to medium, add the red pepper strips and sauté, stirring frequently, until they are limp, about 8 minutes. Add the asparagus and continue to sauté until the asparagus is just tender, about 5 minutes. Add the zucchini and sauté, stirring frequently, until the zucchini is just barely tender, 3–4 minutes. Add the salt and pepper to taste and remove from the heat.

4. In a large pot over high heat, bring the water to a boil. Add the 1½ tablespoons salt and the tagliolini and cook until tender, about 2 minutes. Drain well.

5. To serve, place in a warmed serving bowl. Top with the vegetables. Serve hot.

Serves 8

NUTRITIONAL ANALYSIS: Calories 299 (Kilojoules 1,258); Protein 11 g; Carbohydrates 44 g; Total Fat 9 g; Saturated Fat 5 g; Cholesterol 96 mg; Sodium 455 mg; Dietary Fiber 3 g

Fresh Pasta Noodles

LEMON TAGLIATELLE WITH LEMON SAUCE AND SCALLOPS

When preparing this dish, be careful not to overcook the scallops, safeguarding their tender texture and mild, sweet flavor. If bay scallops are unavailable, substitute fresh sea scallops, cut in half, or small fresh shrimp.

1½ lb (750 g) Lemon Pasta *(recipe on page 11)*

1½ lb (750 g) bay scallops or sea scallops, halved

¼ cup (1½ oz/45 g) all-purpose (plain) flour

2 tablespoons grated lemon zest *(see page 119)*

Salt and freshly ground pepper

5 tablespoons (2½ oz/75 g) unsalted butter

½ cup (4 fl oz/125 ml) fresh lemon juice

1½ cups (12 fl oz/375 ml) heavy (double) cream

3 tablespoons minced fresh flat-leaf (Italian) parsley

8 qt (8 l) water

1½ tablespoons salt

Fresh flat-leaf (Italian) parsley sprigs

1. Make the Lemon Pasta and cut it into tagliatelle (see pages 14–15).
2. Rinse the scallops and pat them dry with paper towels. In a small plastic or paper bag, combine the flour, 1 tablespoon of the lemon zest and salt and pepper to taste. Shake to blend well. Add the scallops, close the bag tightly and shake to coat the scallops well. Transfer the scallops to a large dry sieve; shake them to remove any excess flour.
3. To make the lemon cream sauce, in a small saucepan over low heat, melt 3 tablespoons of the butter with the lemon juice. Add the cream, stirring constantly, until the cream is hot but not boiling. Add the minced parsley. Stir to mix well. Keep warm.
4. In a medium frying pan over medium-high heat, melt the remaining 2 tablespoons butter until foamy. Add the scallops and sauté, stirring frequently, until they are opaque, 4–5 minutes for bay scallops, 6–7 minutes for sea scallops. Using a slotted spoon, transfer the scallops to a small bowl. Pour half of the lemon cream sauce over the scallops. Keep warm.
5. In a large pot over high heat, bring the water to a boil. Add the 1½ tablespoons salt and the tagliatelle and cook until tender, about 2 minutes. Drain well.
6. In a large warmed bowl, combine the tagliatelle and the remaining lemon cream sauce. Toss to mix well.
7. To serve, divide among individual warmed plates. Top with an equal amount of the scallops, sauce and remaining lemon zest. Garnish with a parsley sprig. Serve hot.

Serves 8

NUTRITIONAL ANALYSIS: Calories 538 (Kilojoules 2,256); Protein 25 g; Carbohydrates 49 g; Total Fat 27 g; Saturated Fat 16 g; Cholesterol 188 mg; Sodium 608 mg; Dietary Fiber 2 g

CREAMY LEMON
FETTUCCINE AND LEEKS

The mild, sweet onion taste of leeks goes very well with lemon-flavored fresh pasta. Take care to follow the instructions on page 121 for cleaning leeks thoroughly.

1½ lb (750 g) Lemon Pasta *(recipe on page 11)*

2 tablespoons unsalted butter

1 tablespoon extra-virgin olive oil

1 lb (500 g) leeks, white parts and 1 inch (2.5 cm) green parts, thinly sliced *(see page 121)*

¾ cup (6 fl oz/180 ml) Chicken Stock *(recipe on page 126)*

¼ cup (2 fl oz/60 ml) fresh lemon juice

1½ cups (12 fl oz/375 ml) heavy (double) cream

Salt and freshly ground pepper

8 qt (8 l) water

1½ tablespoons salt

1 tablespoon minced lemon zest *(see page 119)*

1. Make the Lemon Pasta and cut it into fettuccine (see pages 14–15).

2. In a large, heavy frying pan over medium heat, heat the butter and olive oil until the butter is melted. Reduce the heat to low, add the leeks and cook, stirring frequently, until they are wilted and tender, about 15 minutes. Add the Chicken Stock and lemon juice, increase the heat to medium and simmer until the liquid is nearly evaporated, 7–8 minutes. Reduce the heat to low, stir in the cream and simmer for 5 minutes. Add the salt and pepper to taste. Remove from the heat and keep warm.

3. In a large pot over high heat, bring the water to a boil. Add the 1½ tablespoons salt and the fettuccine and cook until tender, about 2 minutes. Drain well.

4. To serve, place in a warmed serving bowl. Top with the leek mixture. Toss to mix well. Garnish with the lemon zest. Serve hot.

Serves 8

NUTRITIONAL ANALYSIS: Calories 455 (Kilojoules 1,908); Protein 11 g; Carbohydrates 50 g; Total Fat 24 g; Saturated Fat 13 g; Cholesterol 149 mg; Sodium 491 mg; Dietary Fiber 2 g

Fresh Pasta Noodles

$\mathcal{B}$LACK PEPPER PAPPARDELLE WITH WALNUTS

Any fresh or dried broad noodle may be used in the preparation of this dish, though the black pepper pasta adds another dimension of flavor. Serve it with a highly seasoned accompaniment such as a spicy soup.

1½ lb (750 g) Black Pepper Pasta *(recipe on page 11)*

3 oz (90 g) Parmesan cheese, in one piece

8 qt (8 l) water

1½ tablespoons salt

⅓ cup (3 fl oz/80 ml) extra-virgin olive oil

Ground nutmeg

6 tablespoons (1½ oz/45 g) coarsely chopped walnut pieces, toasted *(see page 121)*

1. Make the Black Pepper Pasta and cut it into pappardelle (see pages 14–15).
2. Using a vegetable peeler, cut 32 curls of Parmesan cheese and set them on a sheet of waxed paper.
3. In a large pot over high heat, bring the water to a boil. Add the salt and the pappardelle and cook until tender, about 2 minutes. Drain well.
4. In a large warmed bowl, combine the pappardelle and olive oil. Toss to mix well. Add the nutmeg to taste and toss again.
5. To serve, divide among individual warmed plates. Top with an equal amount of the walnuts and 4 curls of the Parmesan cheese.

Serves 8

NUTRITIONAL ANALYSIS: Calories 377 (Kilojoules 1,583); Protein 14 g; Carbohydrates 41 g; Total Fat 18 g; Saturated Fat 4 g; Cholesterol 87 mg; Sodium 623 mg; Dietary Fiber 2 g

OLIVE PAPPARDELLE WITH PROSCIUTTO AND PEAS

A favorite Italian way of serving pappardelle, this sauce can also be used with any other fresh or dried broad noodles. Make the sauce a day in advance, store it covered in the refrigerator and reheat it while the pasta cooks.

1½ lb (750 g) Olive Pasta *(recipe on page 11)*

1 cup (5 oz/155 g) fresh shelled peas or frozen peas, thawed

2 cups (16 fl oz/500 ml) heavy (double) cream

2 oz (60 g) prosciutto, minced

3 oz (90 g) aged Asiago cheese, freshly grated

8 qt (8 l) water

1½ tablespoons salt

Freshly ground pepper

1. Make the Olive Pasta and cut it into pappardelle (see pages 14–15).
2. In a medium saucepan of boiling salted water, cook the peas until tender, about 4 minutes.
3. In a small, heavy saucepan over medium heat, bring the cream and prosciutto to a simmer. Reduce the heat to low and simmer for 10 minutes. Add the peas and cheese and stir until the cheese melts. Keep warm.
4. In a large pot over high heat, bring the water to a boil. Add the salt and the pappardelle and cook until tender, about 3 minutes. Drain well.
5. In a large warmed bowl, combine the pappardelle and half of the cream mixture. Toss to mix well.
6. To serve, divide among individual warmed plates. Top each with an equal amount of the remaining sauce and a sprinkling of the pepper to taste. Serve hot.

Serves 8

NUTRITIONAL ANALYSIS: Calories 518 (Kilojoules 2,177); Protein 16 g; Carbohydrates 44 g; Total Fat 30 g; Saturated Fat 17 g; Cholesterol 175 mg; Sodium 829 mg; Dietary Fiber 2 g

Fresh Pasta Noodles

BEET FETTUCCINE WITH ROASTED GARLIC SAUCE

Cream, simmered with fresh herbs, moderates the flavor of the mild roasted garlic, providing a subtle complement to the beet-flavored pasta. Experiment with different herbs to change the flavor of this dish.

1½ lb (750 g) Beet Pasta *(recipe on page 11)*

2 cups (16 fl oz/500 ml) heavy (double) cream

3 fresh thyme sprigs

1 flat-leaf (Italian) parsley sprig

3 tablespoons Roasted Garlic Purée *(see page 120)*

1 tablespoon minced fresh flat-leaf (Italian) parsley
   Salt and freshly ground pepper

8 qt (8 l) water

1½ tablespoons salt

2 tablespoons chopped fresh thyme

1. Make the Beet Pasta and cut it into fettuccine (see pages 14–15).
2. In a medium pan over medium heat, combine the cream, thyme sprigs and parsley sprig and bring to a boil. Simmer until the cream is reduced by one-third, about 15 minutes. Remove from the heat. Remove and discard the thyme and parsley sprigs. Stir in the Roasted Garlic Purée, minced parsley and salt and pepper to taste. Keep warm.
3. In a large pot over high heat, bring the water to a boil. Add the 1½ tablespoons salt and the fettuccine and cook until tender, about 2 minutes. Drain well.
4. In a large warmed bowl, combine the fettuccine and cream sauce. Toss to mix well.
5. To serve, divide among individual warmed plates. Top with an equal amount of the chopped thyme. Serve hot.

Serves 8

NUTRITIONAL ANALYSIS: Calories 442 (Kilojoules 1,855); Protein 11 g; Carbohydrates 45 g; Total Fat 25 g; Saturated Fat 14 g; Cholesterol 161 mg; Sodium 482 mg; Dietary Fiber 2 g

CLASSIC TAGLIOLINI WITH PESTO SAUCE

A classic sauce like this Genovese Pesto can be used on a variety of shapes or sizes of pasta, but noodles smaller than tagliolini should be avoided or there will not be enough surface area on the pasta for the Pesto to cling to.

1½ lb (750 g) Egg Pasta *(recipe on page 11)*

8 qt (8 l) water

1½ tablespoons salt

⅓ cup (1½ oz/45 g) freshly grated pecorino romano cheese

2 tablespoons pine nuts, toasted *(see page 121)*

PESTO SAUCE

2 cups (2 oz/60 g) packed fresh basil leaves

6 garlic cloves, peeled

½ teaspoon salt

¼ cup (1 oz/30 g) pine nuts

½ cup (4 fl oz/125 ml) extra-virgin olive oil

3 tablespoons unsalted butter, softened

⅓ cup (1½ oz/45 g) freshly grated Parmesan cheese

1. Make the Egg Pasta and cut it into tagliolini (see pages 14–15).
2. Prepare the Pesto Sauce (see below).
3. In a large pot over high heat, bring the water to a boil. Add the salt and the tagliolini and cook until tender, about 2 minutes. While it is cooking, stir 3–4 tablespoons of the tagliolini cooking water into the Pesto Sauce and place the sauce in a large warmed bowl. Drain the tagliolini and add it to the bowl. Toss to mix well.
4. To serve, divide among individual warmed plates. Top with an equal amount of the pecorino romano cheese and pine nuts. Serve hot.

PESTO SAUCE

1. In the work bowl of a food processor with the metal blade or a blender, combine the basil and garlic. Pulse until the basil and garlic are very finely chopped. Add the salt and pine nuts and pulse several times. With the motor running, slowly pour in the olive oil in a steady stream.
2. Transfer the mixture to a small bowl. Using a spatula, fold in the butter and, when it has been incorporated smoothly, fold in the Parmesan cheese. Set aside until ready to use.

Serves 8

NUTRITIONAL ANALYSIS: Calories 475 (Kilojoules 1,994); Protein 14 g; Carbohydrates 46 g; Total Fat 27 g; Saturated Fat 8 g; Cholesterol 101 mg; Sodium 773 mg; Dietary Fiber 2 g

Fresh Pasta Noodles

FETTUCCINE ALFREDO

A specialty of the Roman restaurant Alfredo all' Augusto, this classic is one of the richest ways to serve fresh egg pasta. For perfectly smooth and creamy results, never let the sauce come to a boil once you have added the egg yolks.

1½ lb (750 g) Egg Pasta *(recipe on page 11)*

4 tablespoons (2 oz/60 g) unsalted butter

3 cups (24 fl oz/750 ml) heavy (double) cream

Ground nutmeg

2 egg yolks, lightly beaten

1 cup (4 oz/125 g) freshly grated Parmesan cheese

Salt and freshly ground pepper

8 qt (8 l) water

1½ tablespoons salt

Fresh flat-leaf (Italian) parsley sprigs

1. Make the Egg Pasta and cut it into fettuccine (see pages 14–15).

2. In a medium saucepan over medium heat, melt the butter. Add the cream, bring to a boil, reduce the heat to low and simmer until the cream is reduced by one-fourth, about 10 minutes. Add the nutmeg to taste and remove from the heat.

3. Stir a generous spoonful of the reduced cream into the egg yolks, then return the mixture to the rest of the cream, stirring well. Add the Parmesan cheese and salt and pepper to taste.

4. In a large pot over high heat, bring the water to a boil. Add the 1½ tablespoons salt and the fettuccine and cook until tender, about 2 minutes. Drain well.

5. To serve, in a warmed serving bowl combine the fettuccine and cream sauce. Toss to mix well. Garnish with the parsley. Serve hot.

Serves 8

NUTRITIONAL ANALYSIS: Calories 649 (Kilojoules 2,726); Protein 17 g; Carbohydrates 43 g; Total Fat 46 g; Saturated Fat 28 g; Cholesterol 281 mg; Sodium 716 mg; Dietary Fiber 2 g

$\mathcal{P}$EARS AND GORGONZOLA CHEESE OVER PAPPARDELLE

The rich, sharp and tangy taste of Gorgonzola cheese is a classic accompaniment to fresh pears. It is essential to use fresh pasta in this dish, so if time is short, buy fresh pasta sheets and cut them into pappardelle at home.

1½ lb (750 g) Egg Pasta *(recipe on page 11)*

4 tablespoons (2 fl oz/60 ml) Clarified Butter *(recipe on page 126)*

2 ripe but firm pears, peeled, cored and cut into ¼-inch (6-mm) slices

1 lb (500 g) arugula, cut into crosswise strips 1 inch (2.5 cm) wide

8 qt (8 l) water

1½ tablespoons salt

3 oz (90 g) Gorgonzola cheese, crumbled

¾ cup (3 oz/90 g) walnut halves, toasted *(see page 121)*

Salt and freshly ground pepper

1. Make the Egg Pasta and cut it into pappardelle (see pages 14–15). Make the Clarified Butter.
2. In a large frying pan over medium-high heat, heat 1 tablespoon of the Clarified Butter. Sauté the pears, turning once, until golden on each side, about 4 minutes. Transfer them to a plate and keep warm.
3. In the same frying pan over medium-low heat, heat the remaining 3 tablespoons butter. Add the arugula and cook, stirring gently, until it wilts, about 2 minutes. Transfer the arugula and butter to a large warmed bowl and keep warm.
4. In a large pot over high heat, bring the water to a boil. Add the 1½ tablespoons salt and the pappardelle and cook until tender, about 3 minutes. Drain well and add to the bowl with the arugula and butter. Toss to mix well.
5. To serve, divide the pappardelle mixture among individual warmed plates. Top with an equal amount of the pears, Gorgonzola cheese and walnuts. Add salt and pepper to taste. Serve hot.

Serves 8

NUTRITIONAL ANALYSIS: Calories 413 (Kilojoules 1,736); Protein 14 g; Carbohydrates 49 g; Total Fat 19 g; Saturated Fat 8 g; Cholesterol 106 mg; Sodium 623 mg; Dietary Fiber 5 g

Fresh Pasta Noodles

$\mathcal{S}$ TRAW AND HAY PASTA WITH PARMESAN CHEESE

Butter and cheese, one of the simplest of pasta sauces, traditionally highlights the beauty of this mixture of thin beige egg and green noodles, whimsically thought to resemble straw and hay.

1 lb (500 g) Egg Pasta *(recipe on page 10)*

1 lb (500 g) Basil Pasta *(recipe on page 10)*

12 qt (12 l) water

2 tablespoons salt

4 tablespoons (2 oz/60 g) unsalted butter at room temperature

Salt

¾ cup (3 oz/90 g) freshly grated Parmesan cheese

1. Make the Egg Pasta and the Basil Pasta. Cut each pasta into tagliolini (see pages 14–15).
2. In each of two large pots over high heat, bring 6 qt (6 l) of the water to a boil. To each pot add 1 tablespoon of the salt and one of the pastas. Separately but simultaneously, cook the pastas until tender, about 2 minutes. Drain the pastas separately.
3. In each of two large warmed bowls, combine one of the pastas, 2 tablespoons of the butter and salt to taste. Toss to mix well until the butter has melted and the pasta is evenly coated.
4. To serve, place on a warmed platter. Top with a sprinkling of the Parmesan cheese. Serve hot.

Serves 8

NUTRITIONAL ANALYSIS: Calories 413 (Kilojoules 1,733); Protein 17 g; Carbohydrates 59 g; Total Fat 12 g; Saturated Fat 6 g; Cholesterol 129 mg; Sodium 796 mg; Dietary Fiber 3 g

Pasta with Sauces

OLIVE LINGUINE WITH SALSA VERDE

The classic, pungent green parsley sauce goes well with any type of thin noodle, fresh or dried. Make the sauce up to 2 days ahead of time and store it in the refrigerator. Let the sauce come to room temperature before use.

1½ lb (750 g) Olive Pasta *(recipe on page 11)*

8 qt (8 l) water

1½ tablespoons salt

1 tablespoon grated lemon zest *(see page 119)*

SALSA VERDE

4 cups (4 oz/125 g) flat-leaf (Italian) parsley, stemmed

5 garlic cloves, peeled

8 anchovy fillets in olive oil, drained

1 teaspoon salt

1 tablespoon Dijon-style mustard

¼ cup (2 fl oz/60 ml) fresh lemon juice

¾ cup (6 fl oz/180 ml) extra-virgin olive oil

¾ teaspoon freshly ground pepper

1. Make the Olive Pasta and cut it into linguine (see pages 14–15). Prepare the Salsa Verde (see below).
2. In a large pot over high heat, bring the water to a boil. Add the salt and the linguine and cook until tender, about 2 minutes. While it is cooking, in a large warmed bowl, combine 2 tablespoons of the linguine cooking water and all but ¼ cup (2 fl oz/60 ml) of the Salsa Verde. Drain the linguine and add it to the bowl. Toss to mix well.
3. To serve, divide among individual warmed plates. Top with an equal amount of the remaining Salsa Verde and a sprinkling of the lemon zest. Serve hot.

SALSA VERDE

1. In the work bowl of a food processor with the metal blade or a blender, combine the parsley, garlic, anchovies and salt and pulse for 30 seconds. Add the mustard and lemon juice and pulse to blend. With the motor running, add the olive oil in a steady stream.
2. Transfer to a storage container or bowl and stir in the pepper. Set aside until ready to use.

Serves 8

NUTRITIONAL ANALYSIS: Calories 437 (Kilojoules 1,837); Protein 11 g; Carbohydrates 43 g; Total Fat 26 g; Saturated Fat 4 g; Cholesterol 82 mg; Sodium 1,025 mg; Dietary Fiber 2 g

Dried Pastas

$\mathscr{S}$ARDINES AND CELERY OVER LINGUINE

If fresh sardines are available, sauté them in a frying pan and use them in place of the canned sardines. Other ribbons or strands can be substituted for the linguine.

3 tablespoons Clarified Butter
(recipe on page 126)

1 lb (500 g) celery (about 8 stalks), cut into thin diagonal slices

3 tablespoons fresh lemon juice
Salt and freshly ground pepper

6 qt (6 l) water

1 tablespoon salt

1 lb (500 g) dried linguine

3 tablespoons extra-virgin olive oil

2 tablespoons grated lemon zest
(see page 119)

36 canned brisling sardines, drained

1½ cups (6 oz/185 g) freshly grated Parmesan cheese

1. Make the Clarified Butter.

2. In a medium saucepan over medium heat, combine the Clarified Butter and celery and sauté, stirring frequently, until just tender, 6–7 minutes. Add the lemon juice and salt and pepper to taste. Stir to mix well. Keep warm.

3. In a large pot over high heat, bring the water to a boil. Add the 1 tablespoon salt and the linguine and cook according to the package directions or until al dente (see pages 16–17), about 9 minutes. Drain well and toss it immediately with the olive oil.

4. In a large warmed bowl, combine the linguine, celery mixture and lemon zest. Toss to mix well.

5. To serve, divide the linguine mixture among individual warmed plates. Top with 6 sardines, tails outward, placing them like spokes on a wheel, and an equal amount of the Parmesan cheese. Serve hot.

Serves 6

NUTRITIONAL ANALYSIS: Calories 637 (Kilojoules 2,676); Protein 26 g; Carbohydrates 63 g; Total Fat 32 g; Saturated Fat 13 g; Cholesterol 85 mg; Sodium 893 mg; Dietary Fiber 3 g

DOUBLE TWISTS WITH GREEN BEANS AND GOAT CHEESE

Two strands of pasta twisted together form gemelli *in Italian. The tiny green beans, haricots verts, can be found in produce shops and at farmers' markets throughout the summer and autumn.*

12 oz (375 g) baby haricots verts or Blue Lake green beans

2 red bell peppers (capsicums), stemmed, seeded and deribbed *(see page 122)*

4 tablespoons (2 oz/60 g) unsalted butter

1 teaspoon herbes de Provence

6 qt (6 l) water

1 tablespoon salt

1 lb (500 g) dried gemelli

2 tablespoons extra-virgin olive oil
Salt and freshly ground pepper

6 oz (185 g) fresh mild goat cheese, crumbled

1 cup (4 oz/125 g) shelled walnuts, toasted *(see page 121)*

1. In a medium pot of boiling salted water over high heat, cook the green beans until just tender, about 2 minutes for haricots verts and about 6 minutes for Blue Lake green beans. Drain the beans, refresh in cold water for 5 minutes and drain well.

2. Cut the bell peppers into strips ¼ inch (6 cm) wide and 2 inches (5 cm) long. In a large frying pan over medium heat, melt the butter until foamy. Reduce the heat, add the peppers and sauté until tender, about 8 minutes. Add the herbes de Provence and the beans and sauté until heated through, 3–4 minutes. Remove from the heat and keep warm.

3. In a large pot over high heat, bring the water to a boil. Add the 1 tablespoon salt and the gemelli and cook according to the package directions or until al dente (see pages 16–17), about 9 minutes. Drain well and immediately toss it with the olive oil.

4. In a large warmed bowl, combine the gemelli, bell pepper and green bean mixture and salt and pepper to taste. Toss to mix well. Add the goat cheese and toss again. Add the walnuts and toss once more.

5. To serve, divide among individual warmed plates. Serve hot.

Serves 6

Nutritional Analysis: Calories 634 (Kilojoules 2,664); Protein 20 g; Carbohydrates 66 g; Total Fat 34 g; Saturated Fat 12 g; Cholesterol 43 mg; Sodium 417 mg; Dietary Fiber 4 g

ORECCHIETTE, SAUSAGES AND BROCCOLI IN BROTH

Serve this hearty pasta soup as an appetizer or main course, using orecchiette or other medium-sized pasta shapes. For a more authentic Italian touch, use broccoli rabe, a robust, pleasantly bitter cousin to broccoli.

8 cups (64 fl oz/2 l) Chicken Stock *(recipe on page 126)*
  Red pepper flakes
1 lb (500 g) spicy Italian sausages
1½ lb (750 g) broccoli, cut into florets
5 qt (5 l) water
1 tablespoon salt
12 oz (375 g) dried orecchiette
  Salt and freshly ground pepper

1. In a large pot over medium heat, bring the Chicken Stock and red pepper flakes to taste to a boil. Reduce the heat to low and simmer for 20 minutes.

2. Using a fork, prick the skins of the sausages. In a medium frying pan over medium heat, cook the sausages until lightly browned on all sides and cooked through, 15–20 minutes. Transfer the sausages to paper towels to drain and cool. Cut into ⅜-inch (1-cm) rounds and add to the stock. Add the broccoli and simmer for 15 minutes.

3. In a large pot over high heat, bring the water to a boil. Add the 1 tablespoon salt and the orecchiette and cook according to the package directions or until al dente (see pages 16–17), about 11 minutes. Drain well.

4. To the stock, add the orecchiette and salt and pepper to taste. Stir to mix well.

5. To serve, ladle into individual warmed soup bowls.

Serves 6

NUTRITIONAL ANALYSIS: Calories 456 (Kilojoules 1,914); Protein 26 g; Carbohydrates 52 g; Total Fat 19 g; Saturated Fat 6 g; Cholesterol 43 mg; Sodium 892 mg; Dietary Fiber 5 g

PASTA WITH ONIONS, SHALLOTS AND LEEKS

Lengthy cooking releases the natural sugars present in the onions, giving this sauce a depth of flavor. Use it to top cavatelli or another medium-sized dried pasta shape or over fresh Potato Gnocchi (recipe on page 24).

⅓ cup (3 fl oz/90 ml) Clarified Butter *(recipe on page 126)*

1¼ lb (625 g) yellow onions, diced

½ cup (2½ oz/75 g) minced shallots

1 lb (500 g) leeks, white parts and 1 inch (2.5 cm) green parts, thinly sliced *(see page 121)*

2 cups (8 oz/250 g) dried bread crumbs *(see page 118)*

Salt and freshly ground pepper

6 qt (6 l) water

1 tablespoon salt

1 lb (500 g) dried cavatelli

¾ cup (3 oz/90 g) freshly grated aged Asiago cheese

1. Make the Clarified Butter.

2. In a heavy frying pan over low heat, combine the Clarified Butter and onions, cover and cook until the onions are completely tender, about 15 minutes. Remove the lid and stir the onions. Continue to cook over very low heat, stirring occasionally, until the onions begin to color and turn slightly sweet, 30 minutes. Add the shallots and sauté for 5 minutes. Add the leeks and sauté, stirring frequently, until the leeks are tender, 15–20 minutes. Keep warm.

3. In a small bowl mix together the bread crumbs and salt and pepper to taste.

4. In a large pot over high heat, bring the water to a boil. Add the 1 tablespoon salt and the cavatelli and cook according to the package directions or until al dente (see pages 16–17), about 12 minutes. Drain well.

5. In a large warmed bowl, combine the cavatelli, onion mixture, Asiago cheese and half of the bread crumb mixture. Toss to mix well.

6. To serve, divide among individual warmed plates. Top with an equal amount of the remaining bread crumb mixture. Serve hot.

Serves 6

NUTRITIONAL ANALYSIS: Calories 682 (Kilojoules 2,863); Protein 21 g; Carbohydrates 105 g; Total Fat 19 g; Saturated Fat 11 g; Cholesterol 39 mg; Sodium 771 mg; Dietary Fiber 6 g

PENNE WITH SHRIMP AND PEPPERS

Fresh shrimp (prawns) and multicolored bell peppers (capsicums) are a familiar combination; what surprises here is the addition of fresh ginger, in place of the more usual — yet also delicious — garlic.

6 tablespoons (3 oz/90 g) Ginger Butter *(recipe on page 127)* at room temperature

2 red bell peppers (capsicums)

2 golden or orange bell peppers (capsicums)

1 green bell pepper (capsicum)

1¼ lb (625 g) shrimp (prawns), peeled and deveined *(see page 123)*

Salt

Cayenne pepper

6 qt (6 l) water

1 tablespoon salt

1 lb (500 g) dried penne

1. Make the Ginger Butter.

2. Halve, seed and derib the red, golden or orange and green peppers (see page 123). Cut each half into lengthwise strips ¼ inch (6 mm) wide. In a medium frying pan over medium heat, melt half of the Ginger Butter. Reduce the heat to low, add the peppers and sauté, stirring frequently, until tender, about 10 minutes.

3. Increase the heat to medium and add the shrimp. Cook, stirring occasionally, until the shrimp turn pink and curl, about 4 minutes. Add salt and cayenne to taste. Stir to mix well. Remove from the heat and keep warm.

4. In a large pot over high heat, bring the water to a boil. Add the 1 tablespoon salt and the penne and cook according to the package directions or until al dente (see pages 16–17), about 11 minutes. Drain and toss it immediately with the remaining Ginger Butter.

5. To serve, in a warmed serving bowl, combine the penne and shrimp mixture and toss to mix well. Serve hot.

Serves 6

NUTRITIONAL ANALYSIS: Calories 482 (Kilojoules 2,025); Protein 26 g; Carbohydrates 62 g; Total Fat 14 g; Saturated Fat 8 g; Cholesterol 147 mg; Sodium 516 mg; Dietary Fiber 3 g

BUCATINI TOPPED WITH GARLICKY SHRIMP

Try substituting fresh scallops for the shrimp in this flavorful dish. Exchange the parsley with cilantro (fresh coriander) or arugula for a different flavor. These little tubes of pasta are similar to spaghetti, which may be substituted.

1   lb (500 g) shrimp (prawns), peeled and deveined *(see page 123)*

6   tablespoons (3 oz/90 g) unsalted butter

2   tablespoons minced shallots

1   tablespoon minced garlic

1   cup (8 fl oz/250 ml) dry white wine

¼   cup (2 fl oz/60 ml) fresh lemon juice

2   tablespoons minced fresh flat-leaf (Italian) parsley
    Salt and freshly ground pepper

6   qt (6 l) water

1   tablespoon salt

1   lb (500 g) dried bucatini
    Salt and freshly ground pepper
    Fresh flat-leaf (Italian) parsley sprigs

1   lemon, cut into 6 wedges

1. In a medium pot of boiling water, cook the shrimp, stirring once, until the shrimp turn pink and curl, about 4 minutes. Drain well and set aside to cool.

2. In a large frying pan over medium heat, melt 2 tablespoons of the butter until foamy. Add the shallots and garlic, reduce the heat to low and sauté, stirring frequently, for 2 minutes. Add the wine and lemon juice, increase the heat to medium and simmer until the liquid is reduced by half, about 10 minutes. Add the minced parsley. Stir to mix well.

3. Reduce the heat to low. Add the remaining 4 tablespoons (2 oz/60 g) butter, one tablespoon at a time, stirring constantly, until all of the butter has melted. Add the shrimp and salt and pepper to taste. Stir to mix well. Keep warm.

4. In a large pot over high heat, bring the water to a boil. Add the 1 tablespoon salt and the bucatini and cook according to the package directions or until al dente (see pages 16–17), about 12 minutes. Drain well.

5. In a large warmed bowl, combine the bucatini and shrimp mixture. Toss to mix well.

6. To serve, divide among individual warmed plates. Garnish with a parsley sprig and lemon wedge. Serve hot.

Serves 6

NUTRITIONAL ANALYSIS: Calories 486 (Kilojoules 2,040); Protein 23 g; Carbohydrates 61 g; Total Fat 14 g; Saturated Fat 8 g; Cholesterol 124 mg; Sodium 360 mg; Dietary Fiber 2 g

RIGATONI WITH ARTICHOKES AND ANCHOVIES

This sauce can be made up to 3 days in advance and refrigerated until ready to use. For the rigatoni, you may substitute any other medium-sized pasta tubes or shapes.

2	tablespoons unsalted butter
¼	cup (2 fl oz/60 ml) extra-virgin olive oil
2	cups (10 oz/315 g) chopped yellow onions
2	teaspoons minced garlic
3	anchovy fillets packed in oil, drained and diced
1	cup (8 fl oz/250 ml) dry white wine
1½	lb (750 g) plum (Roma) tomatoes, peeled, seeded and diced *(see page 124)* or canned tomatoes
28	oz (880 g) frozen artichoke hearts, thawed and cut into quarters
	Salt and freshly ground pepper
6	qt (6 l) water
1	tablespoon salt
1	lb (500 g) dried rigatoni
¾	cup (3 oz/90 g) freshly grated Parmesan cheese

1. In a heavy, medium frying pan over medium heat, melt the butter and olive oil. Reduce the heat to medium-low, add the onions and sauté, stirring frequently, until the onions are translucent, about 8 minutes. Add the garlic and anchovies and sauté another 2 minutes. Add the wine, increase the heat to medium-high and simmer until the wine is reduced by half, about 5 minutes. Stir in the tomatoes, reduce the heat and simmer for 5 minutes. Add the artichoke hearts and salt and pepper to taste. Stir to mix well. Keep warm.

2. In a large pot over high heat, bring the water to a boil. Add the 1 tablespoon salt and the rigatoni and cook according to the package directions or until al dente (see pages 16–17), 11–12 minutes. Drain well.

3. To serve, divide the rigatoni among individual warmed bowls. Top with an equal amount of the anchovy and artichoke mixture and Parmesan cheese. Serve hot.

Serves 6

NUTRITIONAL ANALYSIS: Calories 575 (Kilojoules 2,415); Protein 20 g; Carbohydrates 77 g; Total Fat 19 g; Saturated Fat 6 g; Cholesterol 21 mg; Sodium 640 mg; Dietary Fiber 9 g

PASTA WITH TUNA SAUCE

If casareccia are not available, any medium-sized dried pasta shape such as farfalle, fusilli, gnocchi, conchiglie, or orecchiette or strand pastas such as spaghetti or linguine will work with this traditional Italian sauce.

⅓ cup (3 fl oz/80 ml) extra-virgin olive oil

4 garlic cloves, peeled and minced

4 anchovy fillets packed in olive oil, drained

¼ cup (⅓ oz/10 g) minced fresh flat-leaf (Italian) parsley

6½ oz (185 g) canned tuna packed in oil

¼ cup (2 fl oz/60 ml) dry white wine

¼ cup (2 fl oz/60 ml) Chicken Stock *(recipe on page 126)*

Red pepper flakes

¼ cup (2 fl oz/60 ml) fresh lemon juice

6 qt (6 l) water

1 tablespoon salt

1 lb (500 g) dried casareccia

1 lemon, cut into 6 wedges

1. In a small saucepan over low heat, heat the olive oil. Add the garlic and anchovy fillets and simmer slowly until the anchovies begin to fall apart. Add the parsley, tuna and its oil, white wine, Chicken Stock and red pepper flakes to taste. Simmer, stirring to break up the anchovies and tuna, for 5 minutes. Add the lemon juice and stir to mix well. Keep warm.

2. In a large pot over high heat, bring the water to a boil. Add the 1 tablespoon salt and the casareccia and cook according to the package directions or until al dente (see pages 16–17), 9–10 minutes. Drain well.

3. In a large warmed bowl, combine the casareccia and anchovy mixture. Toss to mix well.

4. To serve, divide among individual warmed plates. Garnish with a lemon wedge. Serve hot.

Serves 6

NUTRITIONAL ANALYSIS: Calories 498 (Kilojoules 2,090); Protein 18 g; Carbohydrates 60 g; Total Fat 20 g; Saturated Fat 3 g; Cholesterol 18 mg; Sodium 614 mg; Dietary Fiber 2 g

LINGUINE WITH CLAMS AND MUSSELS

The flattened strands known as linguine are traditionally served with simple, garlicky clam sauces such as this one, and the dish is all the better for the addition of mussels.

¼ cup (2 oz/60 g) unsalted butter

2 shallots, peeled and minced

6 garlic cloves, peeled and minced

¾ teaspoon red pepper flakes

1 cup (8 fl oz/250 ml) dry white wine

3 tablespoons fresh lemon juice

3 tablespoons minced fresh flat-leaf (Italian) parsley

4 lb (2 kg) cherrystone clams, scrubbed

3 lb (1.5 kg) mussels, scrubbed and debearded

6 qt (6 l) water

1 tablespoon salt

1 lb (500 g) dried linguine

1. In a large, heavy pot over medium heat, melt the butter until foamy. Reduce the heat to medium-low, add the shallots and garlic and sauté, stirring frequently, until translucent, about 5 minutes. Add the red pepper flakes and wine, increase the heat to medium and simmer until the liquid is evaporated by one-third, about 7 minutes.

2. Stir in the lemon juice and parsley. Add the clams and mussels, discarding any that do not close to the touch. Cover the pan tightly and simmer until the shellfish just open, 3–5 minutes. Using a slotted spoon, remove and discard any shellfish that do not open. Remove from the heat and keep warm.

3. In a large pot over high heat, bring the water to a boil. Add the salt and the linguine and cook according to the package directions or until al dente (see pages 16–17), about 10 minutes. Drain well.

4. In a large warmed platter, combine the linguine, clams, mussels and cooking liquid. Toss to mix well.

5. To serve, divide among individual soup plates. Serve hot.

Serves 6

NUTRITIONAL ANALYSIS: Calories 475 (Kilojoules 1,996); Protein 24 g; Carbohydrates 63 g; Total Fat 11 g; Saturated Fat 5 g; Cholesterol 55 mg; Sodium 482 mg; Dietary Fiber 2 g

LARGE SHELLS WITH TOMATOES AND CHEESE

The heat of the mildly spiced tomato sauce will slightly melt the strips of mozzarella, leaving them pleasantly chewy. Large pasta shells may be found under their Italian name, conchiglie.

¼ cup (2 fl oz/60 ml) extra-virgin olive oil

1 lb (500 g) yellow onions, diced

6 garlic cloves, peeled and minced

1½ lb (750 g) plum (Roma) tomatoes, peeled, seeded and diced *(see page 124)* or canned tomatoes

1 tablespoon minced fresh oregano

Salt and freshly ground pepper

Red pepper flakes

6 qt (6 l) water

1 tablespoon salt

1 lb (500 g) dried conchiglie

8 oz (250 g) whole-milk mozzarella cheese, cut into thin strips

Fresh oregano sprigs

1. In a medium frying pan over medium heat, heat the olive oil. Reduce the heat to low, add the onions, cover and cook, stirring frequently, until completely tender, about 15 minutes. Add the garlic and sauté another 2 minutes. Add the tomatoes, minced oregano and salt, pepper and red pepper flakes to taste and simmer for 5 minutes. Keep warm.

2. In a large pot over high heat, bring the water to a boil. Add the 1 tablespoon salt and the conchiglie and cook according to the package directions or until al dente (see pages 16–17), about 11 minutes. Drain well.

3. In a large warmed bowl, combine the conchiglie, onion mixture and mozzarella cheese. Toss to mix well.

4. To serve, divide among individual warmed bowls. Garnish with an oregano sprig. Serve hot.

Serves 6

NUTRITIONAL ANALYSIS: Calories 526 (Kilojoules 2,207); Protein 19 g; Carbohydrates 70 g; Total Fat 19 g; Saturated Fat 7 g; Cholesterol 29 mg; Sodium 417 mg; Dietary Fiber 4 g

 ARFALLINE WITH ZUCCHINI AND MINT

Make this dish with small young zucchini (courgettes), which have no trace of the bitterness sometimes found in larger ones. After grating the zucchini, place them in a strainer until ready to use, so their excess liquid can drain away.

¼ cup (2 oz/60 g) unsalted butter

1 lb (500 g) zucchini (courgettes), grated

6 qt (6 l) water

1 tablespoon salt

1 lb (500 g) farfalline

1 tablespoon extra-virgin olive oil

¼ cup (¼ oz/7 g) fresh mint leaves, thinly sliced

Salt and freshly ground pepper

1. In a medium frying pan over medium heat, melt the butter until foamy. Add the zucchini and sauté, stirring frequently, until it is heated through and just begins to soften, 3–4 minutes. Remove from the heat; keep warm.

2. In a large pot over high heat, bring the water to a boil. Add the 1 tablespoon salt and the farfalline and cook according to the package directions or until al dente (see pages 16–17), 10–12 minutes. Drain the farfalline and toss it immediately with the olive oil.

3. In a large warmed bowl, combine the farfalline, zucchini and butter, half of the mint leaves and salt and pepper to taste. Toss to mix well.

4. To serve, divide among individual warmed plates. Top with the remaining mint leaves. Serve hot.

Serves 6

NUTRITIONAL ANALYSIS: Calories 380 (Kilojoules 1,594); Protein 11 g; Carbohydrates 59 g; Total Fat 11 g; Saturated Fat 5 g; Cholesterol 21 mg; Sodium 267 mg; Dietary Fiber 2 g

LINGUINE TAPENADE WITH BASIL AND TOMATOES

The classic Provençal black olive spread known as tapenade is easy to make at home and will keep for several days covered in the refrigerator. You can substitute one of the excellent commercial brands.

6	qt (6 l) water
1	tablespoon salt
1	lb (500 g) dried linguine
2	cups (12 oz/375 g) cherry tomatoes, stemmed and cut into quarters
3	tablespoons minced fresh basil Fresh basil leaves

TAPENADE

1½	cups (7½ oz/225 g) Kalamata olives, pitted
4	garlic cloves, peeled
6	anchovy fillets, packed in oil, drained
1	tablespoon Dijon-style mustard
½	cup (4 fl oz/125 ml) extra-virgin olive oil

1. Prepare the Tapenade (see below).

2. In a large pot over high heat, bring the water to a boil. Add the salt and the linguine and cook according to the package directions or until al dente (see pages 16–17), about 8 minutes. Drain well.

3. In a large warmed bowl, combine the hot linguine and Tapenade. Toss to mix well. Add half of the cherry tomatoes and all of the minced basil. Toss to mix well.

4. To serve, divide among individual warmed plates. Top with an equal amount of the remaining cherry tomatoes. Garnish with a basil leaf. Serve hot.

TAPENADE

1. In the work bowl of a food processor with the metal blade or a blender, combine the olives, garlic, anchovies and mustard. Pulse until the mixture is a dense purée. With the motor running, slowly add the olive oil in a steady stream. Use immediately or store in a tightly covered container in the refrigerator for up to 3 days.

Serves 6

NUTRITIONAL ANALYSIS: Calories 550 (Kilojoules 2,308); Protein 12 g; Carbohydrates 64 g; Total Fat 28 g; Saturated Fat 4 g; Cholesterol 2 mg; Sodium 955 mg; Dietary Fiber 3 g

FUSILLI WITH GRILLED VEGETABLES

This recipe presents a lot of options. Use other favorite fresh vegetables, including small green (spring) onions, slender (Asian) eggplant (aubergine) or an assortment of summer squashes.

¼ cup (2 oz/60 g) Roasted Garlic Butter *(recipe on page 127)*

1 red (Spanish) onion, peeled

4 small zucchini (courgettes)

2 ears fresh corn, husks and silk removed

2 red bell peppers (capsicums), seeded and deribbed *(see page 123)*

2 green bell peppers (capsicums), seeded and deribbed *(see page 123)*

6 qt (6 l) water

1 tablespoon salt

1 lb (500 g) dried fusilli

Salt and freshly ground pepper

1. Make the Roasted Garlic Butter. Prepare a fire in an outdoor charcoal grill, heat a stove-top grill to medium-hot or preheat a broiler (griller).

2. Grill or broil (grill) the onion, zucchini, corn and red and green peppers over medium coals or on the stove-top grill, turning frequently, until they are evenly marked and tender: the onion about 20 minutes, the zucchini and corn 8–15 minutes and the peppers until their skins are blackened. Cool the vegetables.

3. Cut the onion in half crosswise and each half into strips ¼ inch (6 mm) thick. Cut each zucchini into strips 1½ x ¼ inch (4 cm x 6 mm) thick. Cut the corn from the cob. Peel the peppers and slice them into ¼-inch (6-mm) thick strips.

4. In a large pot over high heat, bring the water to a boil. Add the 1 tablespoon salt and the fusilli and cook according to the package directions or until al dente (see pages 16–17), about 9 minutes. Drain well.

5. In a large warmed bowl, combine the vegetables, fusilli, Roasted Garlic Butter and salt and pepper to taste. Toss to mix well.

6. To serve, divide among individual warmed plates. Serve hot.

Serves 6

NUTRITIONAL ANALYSIS: Calories 421 (Kilojoules 1,769); Protein 13 g; Carbohydrates 73 g; Total Fat 9 g; Saturated Fat 5 g; Cholesterol 21 mg; Sodium 369 mg; Dietary Fiber 5 g

$\mathcal{S}$PAGHETTI WITH SWISS CHARD AND LEMON

Like many simple recipes, this one can be varied in many ways. Substitute other favorite greens such as spinach for the Swiss chard (silverbeet). Add more garlic, if you like, and more or less of the red pepper flakes to your taste.

1½ lb (750 g) Swiss chard (silverbeet), stemmed

4 tablespoons (2 fl oz/60 ml) extra-virgin olive oil

1 tablespoon minced garlic

6 qt (6 l) water

1 tablespoon salt

1 lb (500 g) spaghetti

2 tablespoons grated lemon zest (*see page 119*)

Red pepper flakes

Salt

1. Cut the chard leaves into crosswise slices ¾ inch (2 cm) thick. In a medium saucepan over medium-low heat, heat 2 tablespoons of the olive oil. Add the garlic and sauté for 1 minute. Add the chard, cover the pan and cook until the chard is wilted, about 3 minutes. Stir to mix well. Keep warm.

2. In a large pot over high heat, bring the water to a boil. Add the 1 tablespoon salt and the spaghetti and cook according to the package directions or until al dente (see pages 16–17), about 9 minutes. Drain well.

3. On a large warmed platter, combine the spaghetti, chard, lemon zest, the remaining 2 tablespoons olive oil and red pepper flakes and salt to taste. Toss to mix well.

4. To serve, divide among individual warmed plates. Serve hot.

Serves 6

NUTRITIONAL ANALYSIS: Calories 384 (Kilojoules 1,615); Protein 12 g; Carbohydrates 61 g; Total Fat 11 g; Saturated Fat 2 g; Cholesterol 0 mg; Sodium 486 mg; Dietary Fiber 2 g

MEZZE LASAGNE WITH TOMATOES AND OLIVES

The ideal pasta for this dish is mezze lasagne *—ripple-edged ribbons about twice as wide as fettuccine, which have a wide surface to carry the robust sauce. If it is unavailable, substitute the widest pasta ribbons available.*

2 lb (1 kg) ripe yellow tomatoes, peeled, seeded and diced *(see page 124)*

1 shallot, peeled and minced

3 garlic cloves, peeled and minced

1½ cups (7½ oz/225 g) Kalamata olives, pitted and sliced

¼ cup (¼ oz/7 g) firmly packed fresh basil leaves, minced
    Salt and freshly ground pepper

6 qt (6 l) water

1 tablespoon salt

1 lb (500 g) dried mezze lasagne
    Fresh basil sprigs

1. In a medium saucepan over medium heat, combine the tomatoes, shallot, garlic, olives, minced basil and salt and pepper to taste. Simmer until the ingredients are heated through, about 10 minutes.

2. In a large pot over high heat, bring the water to a boil. Add the 1 tablespoon salt and the mezze lasagne and cook according to the package directions or until al dente (see pages 16–17), about 12 minutes. Drain well.

3. In a large warmed bowl, combine the mezze lasagne and tomato mixture. Toss to mix well.

4. To serve, divide among individual warmed plates. Garnish with a basil sprig. Serve hot.

Serves 6

NUTRITIONAL ANALYSIS: Calories 410 (Kilojoules 1,722); Protein 11 g; Carbohydrates 68 g; Total Fat 10 g; Saturated Fat 1 g; Cholesterol 0 mg; Sodium 846 mg; Dietary Fiber 4 g

FARFALLE WITH CHICKEN LIVERS, SAUSAGE AND SAGE

For the best results, take care not to overcook the chicken livers, which should remain juicy and slightly pink at the center. For a more flavorful dish, make farfalle (see pages 14–15) using Basil Pasta (recipe on page 10).

3 mild Italian sausages

5 tablespoons (3 fl oz/80 ml) extra-virgin olive oil

1 shallot, minced

2 tablespoons minced garlic

1 lb (500 g) fresh chicken livers, trimmed of fat and veins and cut into ½-inch (12-mm) slices

Ground nutmeg

Ground cloves

2 tablespoons minced fresh sage

6 qt (6 l) water

1 tablespoon salt

1 lb (500 g) dried farfalle

Fresh sage sprigs

1. Prick the skins of the sausages with a fork. In a medium frying pan over medium heat, cook the sausages until evenly browned on the outside and cooked through, 15–20 minutes. Transfer to paper towels to drain and cool. Cut the sausages crosswise into slices ⅜ inch (1 cm) thick and then cut the slices in half. Discard any fat remaining in the frying pan.

2. In the same frying pan over medium heat, heat 2 tablespoons of the olive oil. Add the shallot and sauté, stirring frequently, until tender and translucent, about 5 minutes. Stir in the garlic and sauté until tender, about 2 minutes. Add the chicken livers and sauté for 2 minutes. Add the nutmeg and cloves to taste and sauté until the chicken livers are cooked through, about 2 minutes longer. Add the sausages and minced sage. Toss to mix well. Remove from the heat and keep warm.

3. In a large pot over high heat, bring the water to a boil. Add the salt and the farfalle and cook according to the package directions or until al dente (see pages 16–17), about 12 minutes. Drain well and immediately toss it with the remaining 3 tablespoons olive oil.

4. In a large warmed bowl, combine the sausage mixture and farfalle. Toss to mix well.

5. To serve, divide among individual warmed plates. Garnish with a sage sprig. Serve hot.

Serves 6

NUTRITIONAL ANALYSIS: Calories 616 (Kilojoules 2,589); Protein 32 g; Carbohydrates 61 g; Total Fat 26 g; Saturated Fat 7 g; Cholesterol 365 mg; Sodium 707 mg; Dietary Fiber 2 g

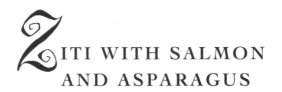

ZITI WITH SALMON AND ASPARAGUS

Salmon and asparagus, classic companions, make a wonderful, simple pasta topping. Any other medium-sized dried pasta tubes such as penne, tubetti or other shapes of the same size will also work well in this recipe.

3 tablespoons Clarified Butter *(recipe on page 126)*

1½ lb (750 g) salmon fillet, skin removed

¼ cup (2 fl oz/60 ml) fresh lemon juice

1 lb (500 g) asparagus, cut into 1-inch (2.5-cm) pieces

12 green (spring) onions, green and white parts, cut into 1-inch (2.5-cm) pieces

2 tablespoons grated lemon zest *(see page 119)*

Salt and freshly ground pepper

6 qt (6 l) water

1 tablespoon salt

1 lb (500 g) dried ziti

1 tablespoon extra-virgin olive oil

2 cups (8 oz/250 g) dried bread crumbs *(see page 118)*

1. Make the Clarified Butter.
2. On a cutting board, slice the salmon crosswise into ¼-inch (6-mm) strips. Place the salmon in a small glass, porcelain or stainless steel bowl, add half of the lemon juice and toss gently. Marinate for 30 minutes.
3. In a small pot of boiling water, cook the asparagus until tender-crisp, about 6 minutes. Drain well.
4. In a medium frying pan over medium heat, melt the Clarified Butter. Add the green onions and sauté, stirring frequently, until tender, about 4 minutes. Add the asparagus and sauté another 2 minutes. Increase the heat to high, add the salmon and stir gently until the salmon just begins to turn opaque. Add the remaining lemon juice, lemon zest and salt and pepper to taste. Remove from the heat and keep warm.
5. In a large pot over high heat, bring the water to a boil. Add the 1 tablespoon salt and the ziti and cook according to the package directions or until al dente (see pages 16–17), 8–10 minutes. Drain the ziti and toss it immediately with the olive oil.
6. In a large warmed bowl, combine the ziti, salmon mixture and half of the bread crumbs. Toss to mix well.
7. To serve, divide among individual warmed plates. Top with an equal amount of the remaining bread crumbs. Serve hot.

Serves 6

NUTRITIONAL ANALYSIS: Calories 624 (Kilojoules 2,619); Protein 37 g; Carbohydrates 76 g; Total Fat 18 g; Saturated Fat 6 g; Cholesterol 79 mg; Sodium 483 mg; Dietary Fiber 4 g

$\mathcal{S}$PAGHETTI WITH OLIVE OIL, GARLIC AND RED PEPPER

A classic and absolutely simple recipe, this spicy dish will fill your kitchen with the aromas of an authentic Italian trattoria. Any other thin strands of dried pasta may be substituted for the spaghetti.

⅓ cup (3 fl oz/80 ml) extra-virgin olive oil

6 garlic cloves, peeled and minced

6 qt (6 l) water

1 tablespoon salt

1 lb (500 g) dried spaghetti
Red pepper flakes
Salt

1. In a small saucepan over low heat, heat the olive oil. Add the garlic and sauté, stirring frequently, until tender, about 5 minutes.

2. In a large pot over high heat, bring the water to a boil. Add the 1 tablespoon salt and the spaghetti and cook according to the package directions or until al dente (see pages 16–17), about 7 minutes. Drain well.

3. In a large warmed bowl, combine the spaghetti, olive oil and garlic mixture and red pepper flakes and salt to taste. Toss to mix well.

4. To serve, divide among individual warmed plates. Serve hot.

Serves 6

NUTRITIONAL ANALYSIS: Calories 391 (Kilojoules 1,641); Protein 10 g; Carbohydrates 58 g; Total Fat 14 g; Saturated Fat 2 g; Cholesterol 0 mg; Sodium 264 mg; Dietary Fiber 2 g

ROTELLE WITH SAUSAGE AND ZUCCHINI

Round rotelle nicely match the size and shape of the sausage and zucchini (courgette) slices. For a milder version of the dish, use sweet Italian sausage, omit the red pepper flakes and add the black pepper sparingly.

1 lb (500 g) hot Italian sausage

1 cup (8 fl oz/250 ml) plus 4 qt (4 l) water

1 cup (8 fl oz/250 ml) dry white wine

1 tablespoon unsalted butter

2 tablespoons extra-virgin olive oil

1 lb (500 g) zucchini (courgettes), cut into slices ¼ inch (6 mm) thick

2 teaspoons salt

8 oz (250 g) dried rotelle

Salt and freshly ground pepper

Red pepper flakes

1. In a heavy medium frying pan over high heat, arrange the sausages in a single layer. Add the 1 cup (8 fl oz/ 250 ml) water and wine and bring to a boil. Reduce the heat and simmer the sausages, turning once, until almost cooked through, about 15 minutes. Using tongs, remove the sausages from the liquid and set on paper towels to drain and cool. Increase the heat under the liquid to reduce to about 1 tablespoon. Cut the sausages into slices ¼ inch (6 mm) thick.

2. In the same frying pan over high heat, melt the butter. Add 1 tablespoon of the olive oil, zucchini and sausages and cook, stirring frequently until the zucchini is tender-crisp and the sausage slices are no longer pink, 7–10 minutes. Remove from the heat and keep warm.

3. In a large pot over high heat, bring the 4 qt (4 l) water to a boil. Add the 2 teaspoons salt and the rotelle and cook according to the package directions or until al dente (see pages 16–17), about 12 minutes. Drain the rotelle and toss it immediately with the remaining 1 tablespoon of the olive oil.

4. In a large warmed bowl, combine the rotelle, zucchini, sausages and salt, pepper and red pepper flakes to taste. Toss to mix well.

5. To serve, divide among individual warmed plates. Serve hot.

Serves 6

NUTRITIONAL ANALYSIS: Calories 471 (Kilojoules 1,978); Protein 17 g; Carbohydrates 31 g; Total Fat 31 g; Saturated Fat 10 g; Cholesterol 63 mg; Sodium 689 mg; Dietary Fiber 1 g

SPINACH SPAGHETTI WITH BOLOGNESE SAUCE

Dried spinach spaghetti, available in most major food stores, provides excellent contrasts of color and taste to this flavorful red meat sauce. If you can't find it, substitute regular spaghetti or other dried pasta strands.

6 qt (6 l) water

1 tablespoon salt

1 lb (500 g) dried spinach spaghetti

¾ cup (3 oz/90 g) freshly grated Parmesan cheese

BOLOGNESE SAUCE

3 tablespoons pure olive oil

1 yellow onion, peeled and diced

1 celery stalk, finely chopped

1 small carrot, peeled and finely chopped

1 lb (500 g) lean ground (minced) beef

¾ cup (6 fl oz/180 ml) milk

¾ cup (6 fl oz/180 ml) dry white wine

3 lb (1.5 kg) plum (Roma) tomatoes, peeled, seeded and diced *(see page 124)* or 28 oz (875 g) canned tomatoes

6 oz (185 g) canned tomato sauce

   Ground nutmeg

   Salt

   Red pepper flakes

1. Prepare the Bolognese Sauce (see below).

2. In a large pot over high heat, bring the water to a boil. Add the salt and the spaghetti and cook according to the package directions or until al dente (see pages 16–17), about 9 minutes. Drain well.

3. If it is not hot, heat the Bolognese Sauce in a medium saucepan over medium heat.

4. In a large warmed bowl, combine the spaghetti and Bolognese Sauce. Toss to mix well.

5. To serve, divide among individual warmed plates. Top with an equal amount of the Parmesan cheese. Serve hot.

BOLOGNESE SAUCE

1. In a large, heavy frying pan over medium-low heat, heat the olive oil. Add the onion and sauté, stirring frequently, until it is translucent, about 8 minutes. Add the celery and carrots and sauté, stirring frequently, for 10 minutes.

2. Add the ground beef, breaking it up with a fork, and sauté, stirring frequently, until the beef just loses its color.

3. Stir in the milk and simmer until it has evaporated, about 8 minutes. Add the wine and simmer until it has evaporated, about 8 minutes longer.

4. Add the tomatoes, tomato sauce and nutmeg, salt and red pepper flakes to taste. Increase the heat to medium, bring the sauce to a simmer then reduce the heat to very low. Simmer for at least 2½ hours.

5. If not using immediately, store in a tightly covered container in the refrigerator for up to 1 week.

Serves 6

NUTRITIONAL ANALYSIS: Calories 683 (Kilojoules 2,870); Protein 32 g; Carbohydrates 74 g; Total Fat 29 g; Saturated Fat 10 g; Cholesterol 71 mg; Sodium 781 mg; Dietary Fiber 12 g

Dried Pastas

PASTA COILS CARBONARA

This traditional Roman version of carbonara, without the cream, works well with substantial pasta shapes such as these plump coils called cavatappi. *If pancetta is unavailable, substitute regular bacon.*

2	tablespoons pure olive oil
4	oz (125 g) pancetta, cut into strips
4	eggs, lightly beaten
1½	cups (6 oz/185 g) freshly grated Parmesan cheese
3	tablespoons minced fresh flat-leaf (Italian) parsley
	Salt
6	qt (6 l) water
1	tablespoon salt
1	lb (500 g) dried cavatappi
	Freshly ground pepper

1. In a small frying pan over medium-low heat, heat the olive oil. Add the pancetta and sauté, stirring frequently, until golden and nearly crisp, 9–10 minutes. Set aside to cool.

2. In a large warmed bowl, combine the eggs, Parmesan cheese, parsley and salt to taste. Add the pancetta, along with any pan drippings, and stir to mix well.

3. In a large pot over high heat, bring the water to a boil. Add the 1 tablespoon salt and the cavatappi and cook according to the package directions or until al dente (see pages 16–17), about 12 minutes. Drain well and add to the egg mixture. Toss to mix well.

4. To serve, divide among individual warmed plates. Top with pepper to taste. Serve hot.

Serves 6

NUTRITIONAL ANALYSIS: Calories 549 (Kilojoules 2,307); Protein 27 g; Carbohydrates 58 g; Total Fat 22 g; Saturated Fat 9 g; Cholesterol 172 mg; Sodium 958 mg; Dietary Fiber 2 g

ANGEL HAIR PASTA WITH ROASTED GARLIC MEATBALLS

A rich garlic-infused poultry broth bathes the thin strands of angel hair pasta and small meatballs in this light yet satisfying dish. If you wish, substitute ground turkey for the beef and pork in the meatballs.

3 garlic bulbs, cloves separated

8 cups (64 fl oz/2 l) Chicken Stock *(recipe on page 126)*

6 fresh thyme sprigs

1 teaspoon black peppercorns

2 tablespoons pure olive oil

2 large shallots, minced

12 oz (375 g) ground (minced) beef

12 oz (375 g) ground (minced) pork

⅓ cup (3 fl oz/80 ml) Roasted Garlic Purée *(see page 120)*

2 teaspoons minced fresh thyme leaves

1 egg, lightly beaten
   Salt and freshly ground pepper

1 cup (4 oz/125 g) dried bread crumbs *(see page 118)*

¾ cup (3 oz/90 g) freshly grated Parmesan cheese

½ cup (2½ oz/75 g) all-purpose (plain) flour

6 qt (6 l) water

1 tablespoon salt

1 lb (500 g) dried angel hair pasta

1. Preheat an oven to 325°F (165°C).

2. In a small ovenproof pan with a tight-fitting lid, combine the garlic cloves, 2 cups (16 fl oz/500 ml) of the Chicken Stock, the thyme sprigs and peppercorns. Bake until the garlic is soft, 45–90 minutes (see page 120). Cool.

3. In a medium saucepan over medium heat, heat the olive oil. Add the shallots and sauté, stirring frequently, until tender and fragrant, about 7 minutes. Set aside to cool.

4. In a medium bowl, combine the shallots, beef, pork, Roasted Garlic Purée, minced thyme, egg and salt and pepper to taste. Stir to mix well. Add the bread crumbs and Parmesan cheese and mix well.

5. Place the flour in a bowl. Shape the meat mixture into 36 meatballs. Coat each meatball thoroughly with flour.

6. In a small frying pan over medium heat, fry the meatballs in batches, turning frequently, until uniformly browned. Drain on paper towels.

7. Strain the garlic-infused stock into a medium saucepan over medium heat. Add the remaining Chicken Stock and bring to a boil. Reduce the heat to low, add the meatballs and simmer for 7 minutes.

8. In a large pot over high heat, bring the water to a boil. Add the 1 tablespoon salt and the angel hair pasta and cook according to the package directions or until al dente (see pages 16–17), about 4 minutes. Drain well.

9. To serve, in a large bowl combine the pasta, stock and meatballs. Serve hot.

Serves 6

NUTRITIONAL ANALYSIS: Calories 830 (Kilojoules 3,484); Protein 44 g; Carbohydrates 89 g; Total Fat 35 g; Saturated Fat 12 g; Cholesterol 120 mg; Sodium 1,054 mg; Dietary Fiber 3 g

PASTA SEEDS WITH TUNA, CAPERS AND ROASTED GARLIC BUTTER

You can't grow pasta from these seeds! Instead, these small pasta shapes resemble melon seeds, melone *in Italian. If fresh tuna is not available, substitute another firm-fleshed fish such as salmon, swordfish or sea bass.*

6 tablespoons (3 oz/90 g) Roasted Garlic Butter *(recipe on page 127)*

2 lb (1 kg) tuna steaks
  Salt and freshly ground pepper

6 qt (6 l) water

1 tablespoon salt

1 lb (500 g) dried melone

2 tablespoons capers, drained

1 tablespoon grated lemon zest *(see page 119)*

1 lemon, cut into 6 wedges

1. Make the Roasted Garlic Butter.

2. Cut the tuna into 1-inch (2.5-cm) pieces and place in a medium bowl. Add the salt and pepper to taste and toss gently.

3. In a medium frying pan over high heat, melt 2 tablespoons of the Roasted Garlic Butter. Add the tuna and cook, stirring frequently, until the fish is opaque on all sides but still pink in the center, about 7 minutes. Remove from the heat but keep warm.

4. In a large pot over high heat, bring the water to a boil. Add the 1 tablespoon salt and the melone and cook according to the package directions or until al dente (see pages 16–17), about 8 minutes. Drain and toss it immediately with 2 tablespoons of the Roasted Garlic Butter until the butter is melted.

5. To serve, divide among individual warmed plates. Top with an equal amount of the tuna, capers, lemon zest and remaining Roasted Garlic Butter. Garnish with the lemon wedges. Serve hot.

Serves 6

NUTRITIONAL ANALYSIS: Calories 592 (Kilojoules 2,487); Protein 42 g; Carbohydrates 61 g; Total Fat 19 g; Saturated Fat 9 g; Cholesterol 82 mg; Sodium 530 mg; Dietary Fiber 2 g

FUSILLI LUNGHI WITH SHRIMP AND TOMATOES

Found in Italian restaurants the world over, this classic seafood dish is easily made at home. If you like, substitute scallops or chunks of firm-fleshed fish such as swordfish or sea bass for all or part of the shrimp (prawns).

1	lb (500 g) shrimp (prawns), shelled and deveined *(see page 123)*
6	tablespoons (3 fl oz/90 ml) extra-virgin olive oil
2	tablespoons minced garlic
½	cup (4 fl oz/125 ml) dry white wine
1½	lb (750 g) plum (Roma) tomatoes, peeled, seeded and diced *(see page 124)*
2	tablespoons fresh lemon juice
6	qt (6 l) water
1	tablespoon salt
1	lb (500 g) fusilli lunghi
1	tablespoon minced fresh chives
1	tablespoon minced fresh flat-leaf (Italian) parsley
	Salt
	Fresh chives

1. In a medium pot of boiling water, cook the shrimp, stirring once, until they turn pink and curl, about 4 minutes. Drain well and set aside.

2. In a large frying pan over medium heat, heat 2 tablespoons of the olive oil. Add the garlic, reduce the heat to low and sauté for 2 minutes. Add the wine, increase the heat to medium and simmer until the liquid is reduced to 2 tablespoons, about 10 minutes. Add the tomatoes and lemon juice, reduce the heat to low and simmer for 5 minutes. Remove from the heat but keep warm.

3. In a large pot over high heat, bring the water to a boil. Add the 1 tablespoon salt and the fusilli lunghi and cook according to the package directions or until al dente (see pages 16–17), about 12 minutes. Drain well.

4. Five minutes before the fusilli is done, return the sauce to low heat. Add the shrimp, minced chives, parsley, the remaining olive oil and salt to taste. Stir to mix well.

5. In a large warmed bowl, combine the fusilli and shrimp mixture. Toss to mix well.

6. To serve, divide among individual warmed bowls. Garnish with the chives. Serve hot.

Serves 6

NUTRITIONAL ANALYSIS: Calories 495 (Kilojoules 2,078); Protein 23 g; Carbohydrates 64 g; Total Fat 17 g; Saturated Fat 2 g; Cholesterol 93 mg; Sodium 366 mg; Dietary Fiber 3 g

$\mathscr{B}$ASIC TERMS AND TECHNIQUES

The following entries provide a reference source for this volume, offering definitions of essential or unusual ingredients and explanations of fundamental techniques as they relate to the preparation of a wide variety of pasta dishes.

ANCHOVY FILLETS
These tiny saltwater fish, relatives of sardines, are usually found as canned fillets that have been salted and preserved in oil. Imported anchovy fillets packed in olive oil are the most commonly available.

ASPARAGUS
One of springtime's great delicacies, asparagus pairs wonderfully with pasta dishes. Purchase only straight, firm stalks with compact tips; when you get them home, trim off the base ends of the stalks, then wrap the asparagus in a damp kitchen towel or paper towel and store in the refrigerator. Use within a few days.

To Peel Asparagus: To use more of each asparagus stalk, peel the tough skin from the base ends. Using a small, sharp paring knife, carefully cut beneath the skin at the base of the stalk; continue cutting upward in the direction of the tip, cutting more thinly as the skin becomes thinner and ending 2–3 inches (5–7.5 cm) from the tip. Repeat on the other sides of the stalk until it is completely peeled.

BLANCH
The term *blanch* describes partially cooking an ingredient, usually a vegetable, by immersing it in a large quantity of boiling water for anywhere from a few seconds to a few minutes, depending upon the ingredient, the size of the pieces and the needs of the recipe.

BREAD CRUMBS
Dried bread crumbs are easily made at home and may also be found packaged in food stores.

To Make Dried Bread Crumbs: Start with a good-quality rustic-style loaf made of unbleached wheat flour, with a firm, coarse-textured crumb. Remove the crusts. Crumble the bread by hand or in the work bowl of a food processor with the metal blade or a blender. Spread the crumbs on a baking sheet and dry in an oven set at its lowest temperature, about 1 hour. Store in a covered container at room temperature.

BROCCOLI
This popular green cruciferous vegetable, a relative of the cabbage, finds its way into many pasta dishes, most often in the form of its small flowering buds, called florets.

To Cut Florets: Cut the flowerlike buds or clusters from the ends of the stalks, including about 1 inch (2.5 cm) of stem with each floret. The stalks can be peeled of their tough, fibrous outer layers, sliced and stir-fried or steamed until tender.

CHEESES

Many different types of cheese complement the taste and texture of pasta.

ASIAGO Originating in the Italian village of the same name, this firm-textured, piquant cow's-milk cheese is sold both fresh and aged for up to 6 months, at which time it is often used in grated form.

FRESH GOAT CHEESE Most cheeses made from goat's milk are fresh, white and creamy, with a distinctive sharp tang; they are sold shaped into small rounds or logs. Some are coated with pepper, ash or a mixture of herbs, which mildly flavors them. This cheese is also known by the French term *chèvre*.

GORGONZOLA A creamy blue-veined Italian cheese. Other creamy blue cheeses may be substituted.

MOZZARELLA A rindless white, mild-tasting Italian cheese traditionally made from water buffalo's milk and sold fresh, immersed in water. Cow's-milk mozzarella is now more common, although it has less flavor. When a recipe calls for whole-milk mozzarella, study the label carefully; some brands may be made at least partly with skim milk.

PARMESAN A semi-hard cheese made from half skim and half whole cow's milk, with a sharp, salty flavor that results from up to 2 years of aging. In its prime, a good piece of Parmesan cheese is dry but not grainy and flakes easily. For best flavor, buy imported Italian Parmesan in block form and grate or shave just before use.

PECORINO ROMANO This sheep's milk cheese is sold either fresh or aged.

To Grate, Shred or Shave Cheese: In most cases, firm- to hard-textured cheeses should be grated with the fine rasps of a cheese grater or cut into thin shreds with the small holes of a shredder; the finer the particles of cheese, the more readily they will melt. Thin shavings of cheese, cut with a cheese shaver or a swivel-bladed vegetable peeler, make an attractive and flavorful garnish.

CITRUS FRUITS

The lively flavor of citrus fruits, in the form of juice or zest, adds fresh spark to many pasta dishes.

TO ZEST A CITRUS FRUIT

1. Using a zester or fine shredder, draw its thin, sharp-edged holes along the surface of the fruit to remove the zest in fine shreds.

2. Alternatively, using a vegetable peeler or a paring knife, remove the zest, then cut it into thin strips.

3. For finely grated zest, use a fine hand-held grater. Vigorously rub the fruit against the sharp teeth.

GARLIC

Whether used raw or cooked, this pungent bulb is best purchased in whole heads (or bulbs) composed of individual cloves, to be separated as needed. Purchase no more than you will use within 1 or 2 weeks, as garlic can becomes bitter with prolonged storage.

To Roast Garlic: Preheat an oven to 325°F (165°C). In a small baking dish with a tight-fitting lid, place 3 garlic bulbs, loose outer skins removed. Add olive oil to a depth of ½ inch (12 mm). Add an equal amount of water. Add 1 teaspoon kosher salt and 2 small sprigs of fresh thyme to the dish, cover and place in the oven until the garlic has the texture of softened butter when a clove is pressed. It will take 45–90 minutes, depending on the size and age of the garlic bulbs. Remove the pan from the oven, remove the garlic from the cooking liquid, and let cool. Store in the refrigerator for 4–5 days.

To Make Roasted Garlic Purée: Place a roasted garlic bulb (see above) on a work surface. Using your thumb, pull out the garlic root and discard it. Place the cooked cloves, all in a cluster, on their side on the work surface and press down on them with the palm of your hand, easing the cooked garlic pulp out the root ends of the cloves. Using a fork, scrape the purée off the work surface and place it in a bowl. Using the fork, mash the pulp to a smooth purée. Occasionally, a root will remain stubbornly in place. In this case, you will need to pull the cloves, gently, one by one, off the root and squeeze the pulp out of each one. One garlic bulb makes 1–3 tablespoons purée. Store in the refrigerator, covered, for 4–5 days.

To Peel and Mince a Garlic Clove

1. To peel, place the clove on a work surface and cover it with the side of a large knife. Press down to crush the clove slightly; slip off the dry skin.

2. To mince, use a sharp knife to cut the peeled clove into thin slices. Then cut across the slices to make thin strips.

3. Using a gentle rocking motion, cut back and forth across the strips to mince them into fine particles.

4. Alternatively, press the peeled clove through a garlic press.

GINGER

The rhizome of the tropical ginger plant, strong-flavored ginger is a popular savory and sweet spice. Whole ginger rhizomes, commonly but mistakenly called roots, can be purchased fresh in a food store or vegetable market.

To Prepare Fresh Ginger: Before slicing, chopping or grating, the rhizome's brown, papery skin is usually peeled away from the amount being used. The ginger may then be sliced or minced with a small paring knife or a chef's knife, or grated against the fine holes of a small grater.

HERBS

Many fresh and dried herbs may be used to enhance the flavor of pasta dishes. In general, add fresh herbs toward the end of cooking, as their flavor dissipates with long exposure to heat; dried herbs may be used in dishes that cook longer, and measure for measure are much more concentrated in flavor than their fresh counterparts.

HOT PEPPER SAUCE

This bottled commercial cooking and table sauce made from fresh or dried hot red chilies is an acquired taste. Many varieties are available, but Tabasco is the best known brand.

LEEKS

Grown in sandy soil, these leafy-topped, multilayered vegetables require thorough cleaning.

To Clean a Leek: Trim off the tough ends of the dark green leaves. Trim off the roots. If a recipe calls for leek whites only, trim off the dark-green leaves where they meet the slender pale-green part of the stem. Starting about 1 inch (2.5 cm) from the root end, slit the leek lengthwise. Vigorously swish the leek in a basin or sink filled with cold water. Drain and rinse again; check to make sure that no dirt remains between the tightly packed pale portion of the leaves.

NUTS

Nuts are sometimes used to add rich flavor and crunchy texture to pasta dishes.

To Toast Nuts: Toasting brings out the full flavor and aroma of nuts. To toast any kind of nut, preheat an oven to 325°F (165°C). Spread the nuts in a single layer on a baking sheet and toast in the oven until they just begin to change color, 5–10 minutes. Remove from the oven and let cool to room temperature. Alternatively, toast nuts in a dry, heavy frying pan over low heat, stirring frequently to prevent scorching.

To Chop Nuts: To chop nuts, spread them in a single layer on a nonslip cutting surface. Using a chef's knife, carefully chop the nuts with a gentle rocking motion. Alternatively, put a handful or two of nuts in the work bowl of a food processor with the metal blade or a blender and use a few rapid on-off pulses to chop the nuts to the desired consistency; repeat with the remaining nuts in batches. Be careful not to process the nuts too long or their oils will be released and the nuts will turn into a paste.

OLIVE OIL

With its rich flavor, its palette of colors from deep green to pale gold and its range of culinary uses, olive oil deserves its reputation as the queen of edible oils. Extra-virgin olive oil is the finest, with a fruity taste and a low acidity that makes it smooth on the palate when used in uncooked dishes or added to hot dishes at the end of cooking. Pure olive oil has a higher acidity level and is fine for a cooking medium.

OLIVES

A specialty of the cuisines of Mediter-ranean Europe and popularized by them around the world, ripe black olives—cured in combinations of salt, seasonings, brines, vinegars and oils—make a pungent addition to pasta dishes. Seek out good-quality cured olives, such as Italian Gaeta, Greek Kalamata or French Niçoise varieties.

To Pit an Olive: Use an olive pitter, which grips the olive and pushes out the pit in one squeeze. Or, carefully slit the olive lengthwise down to the pit with a small, sharp knife. Pry the flesh away from the pit; if the flesh sticks to the pit, carefully cut it away.

PANCETTA

Cured simply with salt and pepper, this Italian-style unsmoked bacon may be sold flat or rolled into a large sausage shape. It is most often used finely chopped as a flavoring ingredient. Available in Italian delicatessens and specialty-food stores.

PEPPERS

Fresh, sweet-fleshed bell peppers (cap-sicums) are most common in the unripe green form, although ripened red or yellow varieties are also avail-able. Creamy pale yellow, orange and purple-black types may also be found.

To Roast and Peel Peppers

1. Preheat a broiler (griller). Cut the peppers in half lengthwise and remove the stems, seeds and ribs as directed on page 123.

2. Place the pepper halves on a broiler pan, cut-side down, and broil (grill) until the skins are evenly blackened.

3. Transfer the peppers to a paper bag, close it and let stand until the pep-pers soften and are cool to the touch, about 10 minutes.

4. Using your fin-gertips or a small knife, peel off the blackened skins. Then tear or cut the peppers as directed in the recipe.

To Prepare a Bell Pepper: Cut the pepper in half lengthwise with a sharp knife. Pull out the stem section from each half, along with the cluster of seeds attached to it. Remove any remaining seeds, along with any thin white membranes, or ribs, to which they are attached. Cut the pepper halves into quarters, strips or thin slices, as called for in the specific recipe.

PROSCIUTTO

A specialty of Parma, Italy, this variety of raw ham is cured by dry-salting for 1 month, followed by air-drying in cool curing sheds for half a year or more. It is usually cut into tissue-thin slices, the better to appreciate its intense flavor and deep pink color.

RADICCHIO

A leaf vegetable related to Belgian endive, the most common variety has a spherical head, reddish purple leaves with creamy white ribs and a mildly bitter flavor. Other varieties are slightly tapered and vary a bit in color. It is served raw in salads, or cooked, usually by grilling.

SHALLOTS

These small members of the onion family have brown skins, white-to-purple flesh and taste like a cross between a sweet onion and garlic. They are a versatile seasoning in pasta dishes.

SHRIMP

Fresh, raw shrimp (prawns) are generally sold with the heads already removed but the shells intact. Before or after their initial cooking, they need to be peeled and their thin, veinlike intestinal tracts removed.

To Peel and Devein Shrimp: Using your thumbs, split open the thin shell along the inner curve, between the two rows of legs. Peel away the shell, taking care—if the recipe calls for it—to leave the last segment with tail fin intact and attached to the meat. Using a small, sharp knife, carefully make a shallow slit along the back, just deep enough to expose the long, usually dark veinlike intestinal tract. With the tip of the knife or your fingers, lift up and pull out the vein and discard it.

SPICES

A variety of dried spices—derived primarily from aromatic seeds, roots and barks—enhances the flavor of pasta dishes. As their flavor dissipates quickly, buy spices in relatively small quantities; store them in tightly covered containers in a cool, dark place.

SWISS CHARD

A leafy dark green vegetable with thick, crisp white or red stems and ribs, Swiss chard is also known as silverbeet. The green part, often trimmed from the stems and ribs, may be cooked like spinach, and has a somewhat milder flavor.

TOMATOES

During summer, when tomatoes are in season, use the best red or yellow sun-ripened tomatoes you can find. At other times of year, plum tomatoes, sometimes called Roma tomatoes, are likely to have the best flavor and texture;

for cooking, canned whole, diced or crushed plum tomatoes are also good. Store fresh tomatoes of any kind in a cool, dark place. Refrigeration causes them to break down quickly. Use within a few days of purchase.

To Peel and Seed Tomatoes

1. Bring a saucepan of water to a boil. Using a small, sharp knife, cut out the core of the tomato. Cut a shallow X in the skin at the base.

2. Using a slotted spoon, submerge the tomato for about 10 seconds in the boiling water, then remove and dip in a bowl of cold water.

3. Starting at the X, peel the skin, using your fingertips and, if necessary, the knife blade. Cut the tomatoes in half crosswise.

4. To seed, hold the tomato upside down and squeeze it gently to force out the seed sacs. Discard the seeds.

$\mathscr{B}$ASIC RECIPES

One of the joys of preparing pasta sauces is their great versatility. Use these basic sauces to top any kind of pasta or on polenta, rice or mashed potatoes. Another favorite is the Bolognese Sauce featured on page 109.

SUMMER TOMATO SAUCE

Make this sauce with the best quality tomatoes you can find. When fresh tomatoes are not available, substitute 48 oz (1.5 kg) of canned whole tomatoes.

6   tablespoons (3 oz/90 g) unsalted butter
1   yellow onion, peeled and cut into quarters
4   garlic cloves, peeled
3   lb (1.5 kg) tomatoes, halved
    Salt and freshly ground pepper

1. In a large, heavy frying pan over medium heat, melt 3 tablespoons of the butter. Add the onion, garlic and tomatoes, reduce the heat to low, cover the pan and simmer for 20 minutes. Remove the pan from the heat. Remove and discard the onion and garlic. Using a food mill or a blender, purée the tomatoes.

2. Clean the frying pan and return the tomato purée to the pan. Place the pan over medium heat and simmer for 10 minutes. Add the remaining 3 tablespoons butter, 1 tablespoon at a time, stirring until the butter is incorporated. Add the salt and pepper to taste. Keep warm until ready to use.

Makes about 1³/4 cups (14 fl oz/430 ml)

SALSA VERDE

Although this recipe calls for flat-leaf (Italian) parsley to give it its green, other herbs can be substituted. Changing the parsley to cilantro (fresh coriander) gives the sauce a Spanish twist.

4	cups (4 oz/125 g) flat-leaf (Italian) parsley, stemmed
5	garlic cloves, peeled
8	anchovy fillets in olive oil, drained
1	teaspoon salt
1	tablespoon Dijon-style mustard
¼	cup (2 fl oz/60 ml) fresh lemon juice
¾	cup (6 fl oz/180 ml) extra-virgin olive oil
¾	teaspoon freshly ground pepper

1. In the work bowl of a food processor with the metal blade or a blender, combine the parsley, garlic, anchovies and salt and pulse for 30 seconds. Add the mustard and lemon juice and pulse to blend. With the motor running, add the olive oil in a steady stream.

2. Transfer to a storage container or bowl and stir in the pepper. Set aside until ready to use.

Makes about 1¾ cups (14 fl oz/430 ml)

PESTO SAUCE

When basil is abundant in the garden, farmers' market or store, consider doubling or tripling this recipe and putting the extra sauce in glass canning jars. The sauce will keep in the freezer for months, bringing a taste of summer to your winter table.

2	cups (2 oz/60 g) packed fresh basil leaves
6	garlic cloves, peeled
½	teaspoon salt
¼	cup (1 oz/30 g) pine nuts
½	cup (4 fl oz/125 ml) extra-virgin olive oil
3	tablespoons unsalted butter, softened
⅓	cup (1½ oz/45 g) freshly grated Parmesan cheese

1. In the work bowl of a food processor with the metal blade or a blender, combine the basil and garlic. Pulse until the basil is very finely chopped. Add the salt and pine nuts and pulse several times. With the motor running, slowly pour in the olive oil in a steady stream.

2. Transfer the mixture to a small bowl. Using a spatula, fold in the butter and, when it has been incorporated smoothly, fold in the Parmesan cheese. Set aside until ready to use.

Makes about 1 cup (8 fl oz/250 ml)

CHICKEN STOCK

Homemade stock adds wonderful flavor to many pasta recipes. If you must substitute, use lowfat, low sodium canned or frozen broth. If you use leftover parts from a cooked bird, do not roast it with the vegetables.

1 yellow onion, peeled and cut into quarters

1 carrot, peeled and cut into large pieces

1 celery stalk, cut into large pieces

1 leek, white part and 2 inches (5 cm) green part

2 tablespoons pure olive oil

5 lb (2.5 kg) chicken parts (backs, necks, meaty carcasses and wings)

6 qt (6 l) water

1. Preheat an oven to 325°F (165°C).
2. In a large bowl, toss the onion, carrot, celery and leek with the olive oil. Transfer the vegetables to a large roasting pan. Add the chicken parts. Roast until the vegetables are tender and just beginning to color, about 30 minutes.
3. In a large pot over high heat, combine the vegetables, chicken, any pan drippings and the water and bring to a boil. Reduce the heat to medium-low and simmer, partially covered, until the liquid is reduced by half, about 3½ hours. Cool to room temperature.
4. Using a strainer, strain the stock into a large bowl. Refrigerate until the fat on the surface solidifies. Before using, remove and discard the surface fat. Store in a tightly covered container in the refrigerator for 5 days or freezer for 3 months.

Makes about 3 qt (3 l)

CLARIFIED BUTTER

Also known as drawn butter, clarified butter is butter with the milk solids removed, which can withstand higher heat for cooking.

½ cup (4 oz/125 g) unsalted butter

1. In a small saucepan over medium-low heat, melt the butter, skimming off and discarding the foam that forms on the top.
2. Using a spoon, transfer the butter to a small container, leaving behind and discarding the solids at the bottom of the pan. Use immediately or store in a tightly covered container in the refrigerator for up to 1 week.

Makes 6 tablespoons (⅓ cup/3 fl oz/90 ml)

BROWN BUTTER

Also called beurre noisette, *brown butter is made by cooking clarified butter until it is amber, resulting in a nutty flavor.*

½ cup (4 oz/125 g) unsalted butter

1. In a small saucepan over medium-low heat, melt the butter, skimming off and discarding the foam that forms on the top. Continue to heat the butter over medium heat until it begins to brown. Watch it carefully and, when it is a deep golden brown and has a nutty fragrance, remove it from the heat.
2. Using a spoon, transfer the butter to a small container, leaving behind and discarding the solids at the bottom of the pan. Use immediately or store in a tightly covered container in the refrigerator for up to 1 week.

Makes 6 tablespoons (⅓ cup/3 fl oz/90 ml)

FLAVORED BUTTERS

Add herbs and spices to unsalted butter and use it on pasta, breads and rolls. Make these butters ahead and refrigerate for up to 1 day or freeze for up to 1 month before use.

Each recipe makes ¹⁄₂ cup (4 oz/125 g)

GINGER BUTTER

¹⁄₂ cup (4 oz/125 g) unsalted butter at room temperature

1 tablespoon grated fresh ginger with its juice

2 teaspoons grated lemon zest

¹⁄₂ teaspoon salt

¹⁄₂ teaspoon sugar

¹⁄₂ teaspoon freshly ground pepper

NASTURTIUM BUTTER

¹⁄₂ cup (4 oz/125 g) unsalted butter at room temperature

40 nasturtium flowers, stemmed and chopped

1 tablespoon chopped flat-leaf (Italian) parsley

2 teaspoons minced shallots

¹⁄₂ teaspoon honey

¹⁄₂ teaspoon salt

¹⁄₂ teaspoon freshly ground pepper

ROASTED GARLIC BUTTER

¹⁄₂ cup (4 oz/125 g) unsalted butter at room temperature

3 tablespoons Roasted Garlic Purée *(see page 120)*

1 teaspoon minced fresh thyme

¹⁄₂ teaspoon salt

¹⁄₂ teaspoon freshly ground pepper

SAGE AND SHALLOT BUTTER

¹⁄₂ cup (4 oz/125 g) unsalted butter at room temperature

1 tablespoon minced shallots

1 tablespoon minced fresh sage

¹⁄₂ teaspoon salt

¹⁄₂ teaspoon freshly ground pepper

TO FLAVOR BUTTER

1. In the work bowl of a food processor with the metal blade or a blender, combine the butter and flavoring ingredients.

2. Pulse several times until the mixture is smooth. If necessary, using a rubber spatula, scrape the sides of the work bowl and pulse again.

3. Transfer the mixture to a small container, mold or ice cube tray or roll into a cylinder. Cover and refrigerate up to 1 day or freeze up to 1 month.

INDEX

Angel Hair Pasta with Roasted Garlic Meatballs, 113
Artichokes, 82
Arugula, 63
Asparagus, 47, 102
    peeling, 118

Basil Pasta, 10, 11
Beans, green, 73
Beet Fettuccine with Roasted Garlic Sauce, 56
Beet Pasta, 10, 11
Black Pepper Linguine with Radicchio and Pancetta, 44
Black Pepper Pappardelle with Walnuts, 52
Black Pepper Pasta, 11
Blanch, 118
Bolognese Sauce, 109
Bread crumbs, 118
Broccoli, 74
    cutting florets, 118
Brown Butter, 126
Bucatini Topped with Garlicky Shrimp, 81

Chard, 28, 97, 123
Cheeses, 119
Chicken
    breast, 43
    livers, 101
Chicken and Fettuccine with Tomato Cream Sauce, 43
Chicken Stock, 126
Citrus Fruits, 119
Clarified Butter, 126
Classic Tagliolini with Pesto Sauce, 59
Crab and Garlic Butter over Farfalle, 23
Creamy Lemon Fettuccine and Leeks, 51

Double Twists with Green Beans and Goat Cheese, 73

Egg Pasta, 10, 11

Farfalle with Chicken Livers, Sausage and Sage, 101
Farfalline with Zucchini and Mint, 90
Fettuccine Alfredo, 60
Fish
    anchovy, 31, 82, 118
    salmon, 102
    sardines, 70
    tuna, 85, 114
Fusilli Lunghi with Shrimp and Tomatoes, 116
Fusilli with Grilled Vegetables, 94

Garlic, roasting, peeling, and mincing, 120
Ginger, 121
Ginger Butter, 127

Herb Cream Sauce, 27
Herbs, 121
Hot pepper sauce, 121

Large Shells with Tomatoes and Cheese, 89
Leeks, 51, 77, 121
Lemon Pasta, 11
Lemon Tagliatelle with Lemon Sauce and Scallops, 48
Linguine Tapenade with Basil and Tomatoes, 93
Linguine with Clams and Mussels, 86

Meat
    beef, 109, 113
    pork, 113
    prosciutto, 55, 123
    sausage, 74, 101, 106
Mezze Lasagne with Tomatoes and Olives, 98

Nasturtium Butter, 127
Nutritional analysis, 9
Nuts, toasting and chopping, 121

Olive Linguine with Salsa Verde, 67
Olive Oil, 122
Olive Pappardelle with Prosciutto and Peas, 55
Olive Pasta, 10, 11
Olive Pasta Tubes with Anchovies and Tomatoes, 31
Olives, pitting, 122
Onions, 77
Orecchiette, Sausages and Broccoli in Broth, 74

Pancetta, 44, 122
Pasta
    cooking, 16–17
    making fresh, 10–14
    serving, 8
Pasta Coils Carbonara, 110
Pasta Handkerchiefs with Tomato and Butter Sauce, 32
Pasta Seeds with Tuna, Capers and Roasted Garlic Butter, 114
Pasta Triangles with Tomatoes and Basil, 35
Pasta with Onions, Shallots and Leeks, 77
Pasta with Tuna Sauce, 85
Pears and Gorgonzola Cheese over Pappardelle, 63
Penne with Shrimp and Peppers, 78
Peppers, roasting and peeling, 122–123
Pesto Sauce, 59, 125
Potato Gnocchi with Summer Tomato Sauce, 24
Potatoes, 24
Pumpkin Pasta, 10, 11
Pumpkin Squares and Swiss Chard Soup, 28
Pumpkin Tagliatelle with Gorgonzola Sauce, 40

Radicchio, 44, 123
Ribbons and Squares with Herb Cream Sauce, 27
Rigatoni with Artichokes and Anchovies, 82
Roasted Garlic Purée, 120
Roasted Garlic Butter, 127
Rotelle with Sausage and Zucchini, 106

Sage Squares with Sage and Shallot Butter, 36
Sage and Shallot Butter, 127
Salsa Verde, 67, 125
Sardines and Celery over Linguine, 70
Shallots, 77, 123
Shellfish
    clams, 86
    crab, 23
    mussels, 86
    scallops, 48
    shrimp, 78, 81, 116, 123
Spaghetti with Olive Oil, Garlic and Red Pepper, 105
Spaghetti with Swiss Chard and Lemon, 97
Spices, 123
Spinach Spaghetti with Bolognese Sauce, 109
Straw and Hay Pasta with Parmesan Cheese, 64
Summer Tomato Sauce, 124

Tagliolini with Asparagus and Zucchini, 47
Tapenade, 93
Tomato Cream Sauce, 43
Tomatoes, 32, 35, 89, 93, 98, 116, 123
    peeling and seeding, 124

Windowpane Pasta with Nasturtium Butter, 20

Ziti with Salmon and Asparagus, 102
Zucchini, 90, 106